7.95

S0-ASK-305

Everything About
EXCHANGE VALUES
For Foods

How to add . . .
mixed dishes, prepared products,
more variety . . . to your diabetic meal plan

By

Marilyn A. Swanson, M.S., R.D.

Pamela A. Cinnamon, M.Sc., P.Dt. (CANADA)

FOURTH EDITION

UNIVERSITY OF IDAHO PRESS

ISBN 0-89301-083-9
Library of Congress Catalog Card Number 81-53064
Copyright ©1986 by the University of Idaho Press

All rights reserved
Manufactured in the United States of America

Published by the University of Idaho Press
Box 3368, University Station, Moscow, Idaho, 83843-0368
(208) 885-6245

TABLE OF CONTENTS

To Barry, Alyssa, Krista and Sara
for their love, reading numbers and patience

and

To Special Friends
for their continued support and encouragement

INTRODUCTION

The fourth edition of *Everything About Exchange Values for Foods* is a supplement to the standard Exchange Lists for Meal Planning, revised 1976.* This book is designed primarily for people with diabetes who wish to incorporate mixed dishes, prepared items, and a greater variety into their meal plan. We strongly recommend that this book be used by **people who have a good understanding of the standard exchange lists and whose diabetes is well controlled.** This book also provides helpful information for use with an exchange-based meal plan for weight control in the absence of diabetes. Dietitians and allied health professionals will find this book a valuable reference.

Everything About Exchange Values for Foods is presented in three parts. Part I contains general supplementary foods. Part II lists main-course convenience foods, and Part III includes miscellaneous items. Foods are listed by product name, brand or type, household measure, weight in grams, the number and type of exchanges represented, and calories. Inclusion of brand names and manufacturers is added for convenience where necessary and does not in any way imply endorsement. It is impossible to list every product available and to try would result in a booklet of unmanageable size and limited practical use. Therefore, every attempt has been made to group brands and items with similar exchange values together.

Foods containing considerable sugar are indicated by a "♦" preceeding the food name. Diabetics should only use foods with considerable sugar under special circumstances, in small amounts, and with their physician's knowledge. Those persons following an exchange meal plan for weight control only may include limited amounts of items containing considerable sugar. Sugar provides substantial calories with none of the other essential nutrients.

If you plan to use an item not listed in this supplement, read the label carefully. If it has a nutrition label refer to page vi, CALCULATING EXCHANGES FROM NUTRITIONAL LABELS. If it does not have a nutrition label read the list of ingredients. The order of ingredients listed will indicate relative amounts present. For example, if sugar is listed first, there is more sugar present than any other ingredient and this item is not recommended for diabetics. Remember sugar and sweeteners are listed on food labels under many names. These include brown sugar, corn syrup, dextrose, fructose, glucose, high fructose corn syrup (HFCS), honey, invert sugar, lactose, levulose, maltitol, maltose, mannitol, maple syrup, molasses, raw sugar, sorbitol, sucrose, sugar alcohols, turbinado sugar and xylitol. If sugar appears near the end of the list of several ingredients, it is a relatively minor ingredient and may be used with discretion. Pay special attention to the relative amount of fat or oil indicated on the label since these supply over twice the calories supplied by carbohydrates and proteins. If you still have questions after you have read the label, consult a dietitian or write to the manufacturer requesting additional information.

It should be unnecessary to purchase "dietetic" foods with the exception of an artificial sweetener (liquid, granular, or tablet), artificially-sweetened or water-packed fruit and perhaps artificially-sweetened gelatin, puddings, and soft drinks. A great many dietetic foods are available, many of which have confusing and misleading label information. Read the label carefully and make certain you understand what you are buying. Generally dietetic foods are not included in this book. Caloric content of special diet items must be included on the label. Some of these contain as many or even more calories than their sugar-sweetened counterpart!

As a general rule, with the exception of foods rich in sugar, the person with diabetes should be able to enjoy the tremendous bounty of foods available today. Hopefully, this exchange list supplement will enable anyone on an exchange-based meal plan to enjoy food and related social activities to the fullest, and by closely adhering to the prescribed meal plan, reap the benefits of optimal weight and good diabetic control.

*Exchange Lists for Meal Planning. 1976. American Diabetes Association, Inc., 1660 Duke Street, Alexandria, Virginia 22314.

ABBREVIATIONS

amt – amount	fl – fluid	pc – piece	tsp – teaspoon
cal – calories	g – grams	pcs – pieces	var – variable
CHO – carbohydrates	lrg – large	pkg – package	veg – vegetable
cont'd – continued	max – maximum	PRO – protein	wt – weight
dia – diameter	med – medium	sq – square	" – inch
env – envelope	oz – ounce	tbsp – tablespoon	

THE EXCHANGE SYSTEM

The exchange system is a method which divides foods into six basic groups or exchanges. The foods in each exchange group contain approximately the same amounts of protein, carbohydrate, fat, and calories as other foods in that exchange group. Therefore one food in an exchange group can be used to replace another food in the same exchange group.

The exchange system was developed by joint committees of the American Diabetes Association and the American Dietetic Association in conjunction with the U.S. Public Health Service in 1950. In 1976 the Exchange Lists were updated to the following Six Major Exchange Groups:

EXCHANGE	CARBOHYDRATE (g)	PROTEIN (g)	FAT (g)	CALORIES
Milk (based on non-fat milk)	12	8	trace	80
Vegetable (includes non-starchy vegetables)	5	2	0	25
Fruit	10	0	0	40
Bread (includes bread, cereal, and starchy vegetables)	15	2	0	70
Meat				
Lean or low-fat meat	0	7	3	55
Medium-fat meat	0	7	5½	80
High-fat meat	0	7	8	100
Fat	0	0	5	45

The 1976 Exchange Lists are used in this book. The 1976 Exchange Lists were slightly modified in fall, 1986. The major change was an increase in carbohydrate content of the fruit exchange from 10 grams carbohydrate to 15 grams carbohydrate, meaning an increase in calories from 40 to 60 calories per fruit exchange. Presently the exchange prescription for most diabetic patients is based on the 1976 Exchange Lists. If your diet prescription is based on the 1986 Exchange Lists you may recalculate the fruit exchanges in this book to the 1986 fruit exchanges using the following information.

Number of 1976 Fruit Exchange		Number of 1986 Fruit Exchange
(10 g CHO or 40 cal)		(15 g CHO or 60 cal)
1	=	⅔
1½	=	1
2	=	1⅓
2½	=	1⅔
3	=	2
3½	=	2⅓
4	=	2⅔
4½	=	3

For additional information about the 1986 Exchange Lists refer to Exchange Lists for Meal Planning available from the American Diabetes Association, Inc., and its affiliate associa-tions, 1660 Duke Street, Alexandria, Virginia 22314 for $1.25 a copy. Call the Diabetes Information Service Center of the American Diabetes Association, 800-ADA-DISC, to obtain the telephone number and address of your local affiliate.

The exchange groups and amounts used to represent any given food item are somewhat arbitrary. The decision of what exchanges are found in a given portion of a food item is based on the amount of carbohydrate, protein, and fat in a selected amount of food, taking into account the most appropriate exchange group or groups to select for each item. Since the values listed are based primarily on caloric content, foods from standard exchange lists must be relied upon to provide the body with its requirement for vitamins and minerals. For example: 2 tbsp. of sweet and sour sauce are listed as 1½ fruit exchanges because this amount contains approximately 15 grams of carbohydrate. Sweet and sour sauce does not supply the body's daily need for Vitamin C, as could a selection of citrus fruits from standard lists. Since this listing must be considered arbitrary, careful attention should be paid to serving size. Measures refer to standard LEVEL measuring cups and spoons. Approximate gram weights are listed for those who have been instructed to weigh all food items or for those who find it more convenient to do so.

The exchanges listed for a homemade item were calculated from a standard recipe and therefore are only approximate for the recipe you choose. Learn how to convert your own favorite family recipes to exchanges and prepare a file for those recipes you use often. Refer to page 5, CALCULATING EXCHANGES FROM RECIPES.

CALCULATING EXCHANGES FROM RECIPES

The simplest way to prepare home recipes with known exchange values is to select one from a special cookbook that lists exchanges per serving. Many such cookbooks are available through bookstores. "The American Dietetic Association Family Cookbook" is a popular example. (Available from the American Diabetes Association, Inc., 2 Park Avenue, New York, New York 10016. Volume I, $14.95; Volume II, $15.95; postage, $2.50 per volume.)

The bimonthly magazine, "Forecast," also available from the American Diabetes Association for $15.00 per year, contains excellent recipes with exchange values, as well as many food ideas and shopping tips. The $15.00 also provides membership in your state-affiliated chapter of the American Diabetes Association.

You also will wish to convert your favorite family recipes to exchanges. Mealtime should be for total family enjoyment; therefore, special items prepared just for the family member with diabetes should be avoided as much as possible. The casserole, stew, or spaghetti you prepare for the rest of the family can be well suited to the diabetic meal plan, provided you can accurately calculate its exchange value. Since these dishes are usually high in calories, plan to serve them only occasionally and in moderate serving sizes. Maintaining optimal weight should be the goal of every member of the family, not just the diabetic.

There are five simple steps for converting recipes to exchanges. See the example on the next page. (Keep a file for those recipes you want your family to enjoy often.)

STEP 1. List the ingredients in your favorite recipe.

STEP 2. Decide how many servings of equal size it will yield.

STEP 3. Convert each ingredient to exchanges. (Remember that meat and vegetable exchanges are based on cooked amounts and ingredients are listed as raw. As a general rule, one pound of raw meat will yield ¾ pound cooked meat.)

STEP 4. Divide the number of each of the exchange groups by the number of servings. Measure carefully when you serve!

STEP 5. Write down the exchanges from the recipe and the serving size for future reference.

Example: Beef Stew

STEP ONE	STEP TWO	STEP THREE	STEP FOUR
1½ lb. stew meat	6 equal servings	24 oz. raw, 18 med-fat meat exchanges	18 ÷ 6 = 3 med-fat meat
1 tbsp. flour		½ bread exchange	negligible
1 tbsp. oil (to brown)		3 fat exchanges	3 ÷ 6 = ½ fat
½ c. sliced onion		1 vegetable exchange	negligible
6 small carrots		6 vegetable exchanges	6 ÷ 6 = 1 veg
6 small potatoes		6 bread exchanges	6 ÷ 6 = 1 bread

STEP FIVE. One serving of beef stew (⅙ recipe) equals 3 med-fat meat exchanges, 1 veg exchange, 1 bread exchange, and ½ fat exchange.

CALCULATING EXCHANGES FROM NUTRITIONAL LABELS

Many foods now have nutrition information panels on their labels. This information can help you incorporate these foods into your diet. Whenever a food product is labeled with nutrition information it must follow a standard form and include the following information: serving size, servings per container, caloric content, grams of protein, grams of carbohydrate, grams of fat, and percentage of U.S. Recommended Daily Allowances (U.S. RDA) of protein, vitamin A, vitamin C, thiamin, riboflavin, niacin, calcium, and iron. Additional information may be included by the manufacturer. To calculate exchanges from nutrition labels you only need to know the serving size and the grams of protein, carbohydrate, and fat in that size serving. The top portion of a nutrition label with this information is shown below.

NUTRITION INFORMATION (per serving)

Serving Size = 1 muffin
Servings per Container = 12

	Mix	Mix + 1 egg + ½ c. milk
Calories	120	130
Protein, grams	2	3
Carbohydrate, grams	20	20
Fat, grams	3	4

The following steps are used to calculate the exchanges found in a food product that has a nutrition label. Refer to the nutrition label for muffins for this example. The actual procedure is shown on page viii.

STEP 1. Write down the grams of protein, carbohydrate, and fat from the nutrition label. (Use the values for mix and 1 egg and ½ cup milk since that is the way you will eat the muffin.)

STEP 2. Choose a standard diabetic exchange or half of an exchange that is comparable to the food product. (See table on "The Standard Exchange.") Subtract the grams of protein, carbohydrate, and fat found in the standard diabetic exchange from the grams of protein, carbohydrate, and fat in the food product. It is okay to have a small negative or positive number after the subtraction.

"THE STANDARD EXCHANGES"

Exchange	PRO (g)	CHO (g)	FAT (g)
Milk	8	12	trace
½ milk	4	6	trace
Vegetable	2	5	—
½ vegetable	1	2.5	—
Fruit	—	10	—
½ fruit	—	5	—
Bread	2	15	—
½ bread	1	7.5	—
Low-fat meat	7	—	3
½ low-fat meat	3.5	—	1.5
Med-fat meat	7	—	5.5
½ med-fat meat	3.5	—	2.75
Fat	—	—	5
½ fat	—	—	2.5

STEP 3. Now evaluate the grams of protein, fat, and carbohydrate which are left over. If you have large positive numbers of grams of protein, fat, or carbohydrate left over, choose another standard exchange or half of an exchange and subtract again.

(REPEAT STEPS 2 and 3 until you can no longer subtract a standard exchange or half of an exchange.)

STEP 4. Write down the standard exchanges that you have subtracted. Refer to the nutrition label to determine size of the portion. Now you know the approximate exchanges found in the food product. Keep a file of the exchanges that you have calculated for future reference.

STEP 1	STEP 2	STEP 3	STEP 2-a	STEP 3-a	STEP 2-b	STEP 3-b
Information from Nutrition Label	Subtract 1 Bread Exchange	What's Left	Subtract 1 Fat Exchange		Subtract ½ Fruit Exchange	What's Left
PRO 3 g	2 g	1 g	0 g	1 g	0 g	1 g
CHO 20 g	15 g	5 g	0 g	5 g	5 g	0 g
FAT 4 g	0 g	4 g	5 g	−1 g	0 g	−1 g

STEP 4

1 bread exchange
1 fat exchange } equals 1 muffin
½ fruit exchange

EXPLANATORY NOTES

"♦" — Contains considerable sugar. Foods listed with a "♦" are not recommended for frequent consumption for diabetics. Use only under special circumstances, in small amounts, and with your doctor's knowledge.

1 low-fat meat (add ½ fat) — This item contains the same amount of protein as one low-fat meat exchange (7 g) but negligible fat. You may add ½ additional fat exchange to your meal plan; however, this is not recommended if you are trying to lose weight.

Milk exchange — The milk exchange used in this book is the standard non-fat milk exchange which contains 12 g carbohydrate, 8 g protein, and a trace of fat.
1 milk exchange (non-fat) + 2 fat exchanges = 1 whole milk exchange
1 milk exchange (non-fat) + 1 fat exchange = 1 2% milk exchange

Meat exchange — The meat exchange can be interchanged.
1 high-fat meat exchange = 1 low-fat meat exchange + 1 fat exchange
1 high-fat meat exchange = 1 med-fat meat exchange + ½ fat exchange
1 med-fat meat exchange = 1 low-fat meat exchange + ½ fat exchange

Regular — Regular sweetened product. Not artifically sweetened.

"free" — Contains negligible carbohydrate, protein, or fat and therefore, calories. Less than 15 calories in the amount specified.

General Note: — One item listed in two different measures (amounts) may have two different exchange values. For example, 2 tbsp white sauce = 1 fat; ¼ cup (4 tbsp) = ½ bread, 1½ fat. This is because the carbohydrate (from flour and milk) is negligible in 2 tbsp, but becomes significant in larger serving sizes.

(S) — Predominantly saturated fatty acids.

(P) — Predominantly polyunsaturated fatty acids.

(M) — Predominantly monounsaturated fatty acids.

Calories — Calories are calculated as follows:
Milk exchange: 80 calories
Vegetable exchange: 28 calories
Fruit exchange: 40 calories
Bread exchange: 68 calories

Meat exchange:
low-fat: 55 calories
med-fat: 78 calories
high-fat: 100 calories

Fat exchange: 45 calories. They are rounded after addition to the nearest 5. The calorie values of the Standard Exchange Lists, revised 1976, p. 3 are rounded.

I. GENERAL SUPPLEMENTARY FOODS

BREADS

ITEM	TYPE OR BRAND	MEASURE	WT. (g)	EXCHANGES	CALORIES
Bagel	Any	1	65	2 bread	135
Banana Tea Bread	Homemade	1 slice (3x3x½")	50	1½ bread, 1 fat	145
Biscuit, baking powder	Homemade or mix	1 (2" dia)	35	1 bread, 1 fat	115
	Refrigerated	1 (10 in 8 oz can)	20	1 bread	70
Boston Brown Bread	Canned	1 slice (3x½")	35	1 bread	70
Bread, Italian, French, Vienna	Any	1½ slices	30	1 bread	70
Bread Crumbs, grated, dry	Any	3 tbsp	18	1 bread	70
Bread Sticks, thin	Any	4 (9" long)	20	1 bread	70
Bread Stuffing					
Homemade	Homemade	½ cup	50	2½ bread, ½ fat	195
Packaged	Stove Top	½ cup	50	1½ bread, ½ fat	170
Cornbread or Muffin	Homemade or Mix	1 average muffin or 1 sq (2")	45	1½ bread	100
Croissant	Sara Lee	1	25	1 bread, 1 fat	115
Broccoli and Cheese	Le San✳wich	1	115	1 milk, 1 bread, 4 fat	330
Chicken and Broccoli	Le San✳wich	1	130	1 veg, 1½ bread, 1 med-fat meat, 3 fat	340
Ham and Swiss Cheese	Le San✳wich	1	115	1½ bread, 1 med-fat meat, 3 fat	315

ITEM	TYPE OR BRAND	MEASURE	WT. (g)	EXCHANGES	CALORIES
Roast Beef in Wine Sauce	Le San✻wich	1	115	1½ bread, 1 med-fat meat, 2 fat	270
Croutons, no fat added	Any	1 cup	30	1 bread	70
Doughnuts					
Cake type, plain	Any	1	30	1 bread, 1 fat	115
◆ Cake type, icing	Any	1	35	1 bread, 1 fat, ½ fruit	135
Raised or yeast, plain	Any	1	30	1 bread, 1 fat	115
◆ Raised, jelly center	Any	1	65	2 bread, 1½ fat	205
English Muffin	Any	1 whole	135	2 bread	135
French Toast	Homemade	1 slice	65	1 bread, ½ med-fat meat, 2 fat	195
Hamburger Bun	Any	½	30	1 bread	70
Holland Rusk	Any	2 average	15	1 bread	70
Hot Dog Bun	Any	½	30	1 bread	70
Melba Toast	Any	5 oblong or 10 round	20	1 bread	70
Muffin, plain, blueberry, bran	Homemade or mix	1 average (2″ dia)	40	1 bread, 1 fat	115
Pancakes					
Plain or buckwheat	Homemade or mix	2 (4″ dia)	60	1 bread, 1 fat	145
Buttermilk	Homemade or mix	2 (4″ dia)	60	1½ bread, 1 fat	145
Popover	Homemade or mix	1 average	50	1 bread, 1 fat	115
Raisin Bread, no icing	Any	1 slice	25	1 bread	70
Rye Bread					
American	Any	2 slices	45	1½ bread	100

ITEM	TYPE OR BRAND	MEASURE	WT. (g)	EXCHANGES	CALORIES
Party size	Any	2 oval slices (3x2x½″)	30	1 bread	70
Taco Shell, ready to eat	Any	1 (5½″ dia)	10	1 bread, 1 fat	115
Tortilla					
Corn, not fried	Frozen or refrigerated	1 (6″ dia)	30	1 bread	70
Flour, not fried	Homemade	1 (7″ dia)	45	1 bread, 1 fat	115
Waffles					
Made with egg and milk	Homemade or mix	1 (5½″ dia)	75	2 bread, ½ med-fat meat, 1 fat	220
Made with water, no eggs	Mix	1 (5½″ dia)	75	2 bread, 2 fat	225
Frozen	Any	1 round (8 in 13 oz pkg) or 2 sq (12 in 10 oz pkg)	50	1½ bread, 1 fat	145

CEREALS

Note: There is much variation among different cereals. The following gives the quantity of cereal equivalent to one bread exchange when possible. Note the difference in weights. You are encouraged to check the nutrition labels found on many of these products. Some nutrition labels on dry cereal products provide additional information on the type of carbohydrates found in the product. Avoid presweetened cereals, cereals with a large quantity of carbohydrates in the form of sucrose and cereals with sugar listed as the first ingredient.

ITEM	TYPE OR BRAND	MEASURE	WT. (g)	EXCHANGES	CALORIES
All-Bran	Kellogg's	⅓ cup	30	1 bread	70
Almond Delight	Ralston	½ cup	20	1 bread	70
Bran Buds	Kellogg's	⅓ cup	30	1 bread	70
Bran Cereal	Nabisco	⅓ cup	30	1 bread	70
Cheerios	General Mills	¾ cup	20	1 bread	70
Chex					
Bran	Ralston	½ cup	20	1 bread	70
Corn	Ralston	⅔ cup	20	1 bread	70
Rice	Ralston	¾ cup	20	1 bread	70
Wheat	Ralston	½ cup	25	1 bread	70
Wheat & Raisins	Ralston	⅓ cup	15	1 bread	70
Corn Bran	Quaker	⅓ cup	15	1 bread	70
Cracklin' Oat Bran	Kellogg's	¼ cup	15	1 bread	70
Crispix	Kellogg's	½ cup	20	1 bread	70
Flakes					
Bran	Any	½ cup	20	1 bread	70
Corn	Any	¾ cup	20	1 bread	70
Oat	Post	½ cup	25	1 bread	70
Wheat	Any	¾ cup	25	1 bread	70
Fruitful Bran	Kellogg's	⅓ cup	20	1 bread	70

ITEM	TYPE OR BRAND	MEASURE	WT. (g)	EXCHANGES	CALORIES
Granola Type	Homemade or Packaged	¼ cup	30	1 bread, 1 fat	115
Grape Nuts	Post	3 tbsp	25	1 bread	70
Life					
Regular	Quaker	⅔ cup	30	1 bread, ½ low-fat meat	95
Cinnamon	Quaker	⅔ cup	30	1 bread, ½ low-fat meat	95
Raisin	Quaker	½ cup	30	1 bread, ½ low-fat meat	95
Most	Kellogg's	⅓ cup	20	1 bread	70
Nutri-Grain					
Corn	Kellogg's	⅓ cup	20	1 bread	70
Wheat	Kellogg's	⅓ cup	15	1 bread	70
Wheat and Raisins	Kellogg's	⅓ cup	20	1 bread	70
Product 19	Kellogg's	⅔ cup	20	1 bread	70
Puffed Type					
Corn, not sweetened	Any	1 cup	10	1 bread	70
Rice, not sweetened	Any	1½ cup	20	1 bread	70
Wheat, not sweetened	Any	1½ cup	10	1 bread	70
Raisin Bran	Any	½ cup	25	1 bread	70
Raisins, Rice and Rye	Kellogg's	⅓ cup	15	1 bread	70
Rice Krispies	Kellogg's	⅔ cup	20	1 bread	70
Shredded Wheat Biscuit	Nabisco/Quaker	1 biscuit	20	1 bread	70
Special K	Kellogg's	⅔ cup	20	1 bread	70
Wheat Germ	Any	2 tbsp	10	½ bread	35

CHEESES

ITEM	TYPE OR BRAND	MEASURE	WT. (g)	EXCHANGES	CALORIES
American Process Cheese Slices	Any	1 oz*	30	1 med-fat meat, ½ fat	100
Blue or Roquefort	Any	1 oz (2 tbsp)	30	1 med-fat meat, ½ fat	100
Brick	Any	1 oz (1x1x1″)	30	1 med-fat meat, 1 fat	120
Brie	Any	1 oz (1x1x1″)	30	½ med-fat meat, 1 fat	85
Camembert, domestic	Any	1 oz	30	½ med-fat meat, 1 fat	85
Caraway	Any	1 oz (1x1x1″)	30	1 med-fat meat, ½ fat	100
Cheddar, Mild or Sharp	Any	1 oz (1x1x1″)	30	1 med-fat meat, 1 fat	120
Cheese Whiz, cheese spread	Kraft	1 oz (2 tbsp)	30	2 med-fat meat, 1 fat	85
Colby	Any	1 oz (1x1x1″)	30	1 med-fat meat, 1 fat	120
Cream Cheese					
regular	Any	1 oz (2 tbsp)	30	½ med-fat meat, 1½ fat	105
light, processed	Kraft	1 oz	30	½ med-fat meat, ½ fat	60
soft	Kraft	1 oz	30	¼ med-fat meat, 2 fat	110
Edam	Any	1 oz (1x1x1″)	30	1 med-fat meat, ½ fat	100
Feta	Any	1 oz (1x1x1″)	30	½ med-fat meat, 1 fat	85
Gjetost	Any	1 oz (1x1x1″)	30	2 veg. 1½ fat	125
Gouda	Any	1 oz	30	1 med-fat meat, ½ fat	100
Light 'n Lively	Kraft	1 oz (1⅓ slice)	30	1 low-fat meat	55
Monterey Jack	Any	1 oz (1x1x1″)	30	1 med-fat meat, ½ fat	100

*Pre-sliced process cheese is available in 1 oz (30g), ¾ oz (21g) or ⅔ oz (18g) slices. Check the label.

ITEM	TYPE OR BRAND	MEASURE	WT. (g)	EXCHANGES	CALORIES
Mozzarella, part skim	Any	1 oz (1x1x1″)	30	1 med-fat meat	80
Muenster	Any	1 oz (1x1x1″)	30	1 med-fat meat, ½ fat	100
Parmesan or Romano, grated	Any	3 tbsp	15	1 med-fat meat	80
Provolone	Any	1 oz (1x1x1″)	30	1 med-fat meat, ½ fat	100
Ricotta, part skim	Any	¼ cup	60	1 med-fat meat	80
Squeeze-A-Snack	Kraft	1 oz	30	½ med-fat meat, 1 fat	85
Swiss					
regular	Any	1 oz (1x1x1″)	30	1 med-fat meat, ½ fat	100
process Swiss slices	Any	1 oz*	30	1 med-fat meat, ½ fat	100
Velveeta Process Cheese Spread	Kraft	2 tbsp	30	½ med-fat meat, 1 fat	80
Weight Watchers Cheese Slices	Weight Watchers	1 oz slice	30	1 low-fat meat	55

*Pre-sliced process cheese is available in 1 oz (30g), ¾ oz (21g) or ⅔ oz (18g) slices. Check the label.

Note: Since it is impossible to include every item available, a selection of popular crackers and cookies is given. Many of these products have nutrition labels. You can use these to calculate exchanges for yourself. (See CALCULATING EXCHANGES FROM NUTRITION LABELS SECTION, pg 6) Generally the weight of the serving size will be given. You will need to first weigh out a serving size portion of the product and then count the number of items in that weight. Many of the following products are high in sugar and should not be included in the diabetic meal plan. Pay particular attention to the weight of homemade products. A larger or smaller homemade product will have more or less exchanges.

ITEM	TYPE OR BRAND	MEASURE	WT. (g)	EXCHANGES	CALORIES
Animal Crackers	Any	8	15	1 bread	70
Arrowroot Biscuits	Any	3	15	1 bread	70
Bacon Thins	Nabisco	7	15	½ bread, 1 fat	80
◆ Bordeaux	Pepperidge Farm	3	25	1 bread, 1 fat	115
Bugles	General Mills	16	15	½ bread, 1 fat	80
Cheese Puffs or Balls	Any	1 oz*	30	1 bread, 2 fat	160
Cheese Tid-Bits	Nabisco	16	15	½ bread, 1 fat	80
Chicken in a Biskit	Nabisco	7	15	½ bread, 1 fat	80
◆ Chocolate Chip Cookies	Homemade	2	25	1 bread, 1 fat	115
◆ Chocolate Covered Grahams	Any	2	25	1 bread, 1 fat	115
◆ Chocolate Sandwich Cookies	Any	2	20	1 bread, 1 fat	115
Corn Chips, plain or flavored	Any	1 oz*	30	1 bread, 2 fat	160
◆ Fig Newtons	Any	2	30	1½ bread	100
Fruit Roll-ups, any flavor	General Mills	¾ roll	10	1 fruit	40
Gingersnaps, Lemon Snaps	Any	4 small	15	1 bread	70

*This product comes in many sizes, shapes and flavors. Generally the exchanges are similar by weight. To determine the number of pieces in a given exchange, weigh the measure and count the pieces.

ITEM	TYPE OR BRAND	MEASURE	WT. (g)	EXCHANGES	CALORIES
◆ Granola Bars	Nature Valley	1	25	½ fruit, 1 bread, 1 fat	135
Granola Snack Bars, New Trail					
◆ Apple	Hershey	1 (1.4 oz)	40	1½ bread, 2 fat	195
◆ Cinnamon	Hershey	1 (1.4 oz)	40	1½ bread, 2 fat	195
◆ Honey Graham	Hershey	1 (1.4 oz)	40	½ fruit, 1½ bread, 2 fat	215
◆ Peanut Butter	Hershey	1 (1.4 oz)	40	½ veg, 2 fruit, ½ med-fat meat, 1½ fat	200
◆ Peanut Butter & Choc. Chip	Hershey	1 (1.4 oz)	40	½ veg, 2 fruit, ½ med-fat meat, 1½ fat	200
Graham Crackers	Any	2 (2½″ sq)	15	1 bread	70
Handi-Snacks					
Cheez'n Crackers	Kraft	1 pkg (⅜ oz)	10	½ bread, ½ med-fat meat, 1 fat	120
Peanut Butter'n Cheez Crackers	Kraft	1 pkg (⅜ oz)	10	1 veg, ½ bread, ½ med-fat meat, 2 fat	190
Ladyfingers	Any	1½ large	20	1 bread	70
◆ Lido	Pepperidge Farm	1½	25	1 bread, 1½ fat	135
◆ Lorna Doone Shortbread	Nabisco	3	25	1 bread, 1 fat	115
Matzoh	Any	1 (6″ dia)	20	1 bread	70
◆ Milano	Pepperidge Farm	1	10	½ bread, ½ fat	55
◆ Oatmeal Cookies	Homemade	1	15	½ bread, ½ fat	55
◆ Orleans	Pepperidge Farm	1	10	½ bread, ½ fat	55
Oyster Crackers	Any	25	20	1 bread, ½ fat	90
Popcorn, popped, no fat added	Any	1½ cup	20	1 bread	70

ITEM	TYPE OR BRAND	MEASURE	WT. (g)	EXCHANGES	CALORIES
Popcorn, popped, flavored	Microwave	2 cup	30	1 bread, 1½ fat	135
Potato Chips	Any	1 oz*	30	1 bread, 2 fat	160
Pretzels	Any	⅔ oz*	20	1 bread	70
Refrigerator Cookies/Brownies					
◆ Chocolate Chip	Pillsbury	2	30	1 fruit, ½ bread, 1 fat	120
◆ Double Chocolate	Pillsbury	2	30	1½ fruit, 1 fat	105
◆ Fudge Brownies	Pillsbury	1	30	1½ fruit, ½ fat	180
◆ Oatmeal Raisin	Pillsbury	2	30	1 bread, 1 fat	115
◆ Peanut Butter	Pillsbury	2	30	1 bread, 1½ fat	135
◆ Sugar	Pillsbury	2	30	1 fruit, ½ bread, 1 fat	120
Ritz Crackers, plain or cheese	Nabisco	7	25	1 bread, 1 fat	115
◆ Rochelle	Pepperidge Farm	1	15	½ bread, 1 fat	80
Ry-Krisp	Any	3 (36 in 1 lb)	20	1 bread	70
Saltines	Any	6	20	1 bread	70
◆ Sandwich Cookies, creme filled	Any	2	20	1 bread, 1 fat	115
Sociables	Nabisco	12	25	1 bread, 1 fat	115
Social Tea Biscuits	Nabisco	3	15	1 bread	70
◆ Sugar Cookies	Homemade	1	20	1 bread, ½ fat	90
◆ Sugar Wafers	Any	5	25	1 bread, 1 fat	115
Tortilla Chips	Any	1 oz*	30	1 bread, 1½ fat	135

*This product comes in many sizes, shapes and flavors. Generally the exchanges are similar by weight. To determine the number of pieces in a given exchange, weigh the measure and count the pieces.

ITEM	TYPE OR BRAND	MEASURE	WT. (g)	EXCHANGES	CALORIES
Triscuit Wafers	Nabisco	3	15	1 bread	70
Vanilla Wafers	Nabisco	4	15	1 bread	70
Vegetable Thins	Nabisco	12	20	1 bread, 1 fat	115
Waverly Wafers	Nabisco	6	25	1 bread, 1 fat	115
Wheat Thins	Nabisco	12	20	1 bread, 1 fat	115
Zweibach	Any	2	60	1 bread	70

ITEM	TYPE OR BRAND	MEASURE	WT. (g)	EXCHANGES	CALORIES
◆ Apple Crisp	Homemade	½ cup	145	5 fruit, ½ bread, 1½ fat	300
Brownies					
◆ Plain, not iced	Homemade or mix	1 (2x2x¾″)	30	1 bread, 2 fat	160
◆ Plain, with icing	Frozen	1 (2x2x1″)	30	1 bread, 1 fat	115
Cake					
Angel Food, no icing	Homemade or mix	½₀ (1½″)	25	1 bread	70
◆ Cupcake, no icing	Homemade or mix	1	40	1½ bread, 1 fat	145
◆ Mix, most flavors, no icing	Any	¹⁄₁₂ (2 layer)	50	2½ bread, 1 fat	215
◆ Pound cake, no icing	Homemade or mix	1 (3x3x½″)	30	1 bread, 1 fat	115
◆ Sponge cake, no icing	Homemade	½₀ (1½″)	25	1 bread	70
Cream Puff, shell only	Homemade	1 average (6 from ½ cup flour)	15	½ bread, ½ med-fat meat, 1½ fat	140
Custard					
◆ Baked, regular, non-fat milk	Homemade or mix	½ cup	150	½ milk, ½ bread, ½ fat	95
◆ Baked, regular, whole milk	Homemade or mix	½ cup	150	1 milk, ½ bread, 2 fat	205
Danish Pastries					
◆ Apple	Sara Lee	1	35	½ fruit, 1 bread, 1 fat	135
◆ Cheese	Sara Lee	1	35	1 bread, 1½ fat	135
◆ Plain	Homemade	1	40	½ fruit, 1 bread, 1 fat	135
◆ Refrigerated	Pillsbury	1	40	½ fruit, 1 bread, 1 fat	135
Fruit 'N Juice Bars	Dole	1	70	1½ fruit	60
Gelatin Dessert					
◆ Regular	Any	⅓ cup (6 in 3 oz pkg)	95	1 bread	70
Artifically sweetened	Jello	½ cup	140	free	
◆ Gelatin Pops	Jello	1 (1¾ oz)	50	1 fruit	40

ITEM	TYPE OR BRAND	MEASURE	WT. (g)	EXCHANGES	CALORIES
Ice Cream					
♦ Regular	Any	½ cup	70	1 bread, 2 fat	160
♦ Soft	Any	⅓ cup	40	1 bread, 1½ fat	135
♦ Ice Milk	Any	½ cup	70	1 bread, 1 fat	115
♦ Peach Cobbler	Homemade	⅓ cup	100	1½ fruit, ½ bread, 1½ fat	160
Piecrust, shell only					
♦ Graham Cracker (margarine and sugar added)	Any	⅛ of 9" pie	20	½ bread, 1½ fat	100
♦ Pastry, 1 crust	Homemade, mix or frozen	⅛ of 9" pie	15	½ bread, 1 fat	80
Pies					
♦ Cream pies, frozen	Any	⅛ of 10 oz pie	35	1 bread, 1 fat	115
♦ Fruit pies, frozen	Any	⅛ of 20 oz pie	70	2 bread, 1½ fat	205
♦ Popsicle, any flavor	Any	1 twin bar	90	2 fruit	80
Pudding					
Artificially sweetened, made with 2% milk	Jello	½ cup	130	½ milk, 1½ fruit	100
♦ Regular, cooked and instant made with non-fat milk	Any	½ cup	140	½ milk, 1½ bread	140
♦ Regular, cooked and instant made with whole milk	Any	½ cup	140	½ milk, 1½ bread, 1 fat	185
♦ Regular, lemon	Any	½ cup	140	1½ bread	100
♦ Pudding Pops	Jello	1 (1¾ oz)	50	1 bread, ½ fat	90
♦ Sherbet, any flavor	Any	½ cup	100	2 bread	135
♦ Turnovers	Pillsbury	1	85	1 fruit, 1 bread, 1½ fat	175
♦ Yogurt, frozen, fruit varieties	Any	½ cup	115	½ milk, 1½ fruit	100

ITEM	TYPE OR BRAND	MEASURE	WT. (g)	EXCHANGES	CALORIES
Avocado	Fresh	⅛ (4″ dia)	25	1 fat (P)	45
◆ Chocolate, chips, semi-sweet	Any	⅙ cup	30	1 bread, 1½ fat (S)	135
Coffee Cream Substitute*					
Powdered	Any	2 level tsp	5	½ fat (S)	25
Frozen, liquid	Any	2 tbsp	30	1 fat (S)	45
Coconut	Fresh	1 piece (1x1x⅜″)	15	1 fat (S)	45
◆ Dried, shredded, sweetened	Any	2-3 tbsp	15	½ fruit, 1 fat (S)	45
Diet Margarine (water added)	Any	2 tsp	10	1 fat (P)	45
Dips, ready-to-serve	Any	2 tbsp	30	1 fat (S)	45
Gravy (see also "Sauces")	Homemade	2 tbsp	35	1 fat (S)	45
Mayonnaise	Any	½ tbsp	10	1 fat (S)	45
Olives					
Green	Any	10 med	40	1 fat (M)	45
Ripe, black	Any	6 med	25	1 fat (M)	45
Salad Dressings, regular					
Blue Cheese	Any	2 tsp	10	1 fat (P)	45
Caesar	Any	2 tsp	10	1 fat (P)	45
French	Any	2 tsp	10	1 fat (P)	45
Green Goddess	Any	2 tsp	10	1 fat (P)	45
Homemade, cooked, boiled	Any	3 tbsp	45	1 veg, 1 fat (P)	70

*Contains more carbohydrate than natural cream.

ITEM	TYPE OR BRAND	MEASURE	WT. (g)	EXCHANGES	CALORIES
Italian	Any	2 tsp	10	1 fat (P)	45
Italian, creamy	Any	1 tbsp	15	1 fat (P)	45
"Mayonnaise-type" Salad Dressing	Any	2 tsp	10	1 fat (P)	45
Thousand Island	Any	2 tsp	10	1 fat (P)	45
Salad Dressings, reduced calories					
Bacon & Tomato	Kraft	2 tbsp	30	½ fruit, 1 fat	65
Catalina	Kraft	1 tbsp	15	free	15
Chunky Blue Cheese	Kraft	2 tbsp	30	½ fruit, 1 fat	65
Creamy Bacon	Kraft	2 tbsp	30	½ fruit, 1 fat	65
Creamy Buttermilk	Kraft	1½ tbsp	25	1 fat	45
Creamy Cucumber	Kraft	1½ tbsp	25	1 fat	45
Creamy Italian	Kraft	2 tbsp	30	1 fat	45
French	Kraft	2 tbsp	30	1 fat	45
Italian	Kraft	1 tbsp	15	free	5
Roka Brand Blue Cheese	Kraft	1 tbsp	15	free	15
Russian	Kraft	2 tbsp	30	1 fruit, ½ fat	65
Thousand Island	Kraft	2 tbsp	30	½ fruit, 1 fat	65
Salad Dressing Mix, prepared	Good Seasons	1 tbsp	15	2 fat (P)	90
Sandwich Spread	Kraft, Hellman's*	2 tsp	10	1 fat (P)	45
Sour Cream	Any	2 tbsp	30	1 fat (S)	45
Sour Dressing (non-fat dry milk & vegetable fat)	Imo	2 tbsp	30	1 fat (S)	45
Sour Half and Half	Any	3 tbsp	45	1 fat (S)	45

*Hellman's is called Best Foods west of the Rockies.

FATS

ITEM	TYPE OR BRAND	MEASURE	WT. (g)	EXCHANGES	CALORIES
Tartar Sauce	Bottled or mix	2 tsp	15	1 fat (P)	45
Whipped Cream, artificially sweetened	Homemade	1 tbsp unwhipped or 2 tbsp whipped	15	1 fat (S)	45
Whipped Topping					
Artificially sweetened	D'Zerta	5 tbsp max	20	free (S)	15
Aerosol, regular	Ready Whip	5 tbsp	20	1 fat (S)	45
		1 tbsp	5	free (S)	15
Frozen, regular	Rich's Spoon 'n Serve	5 tbsp	20	½ fruit, 1 fat (S)	65
	Cool Whip	1 tbsp	5	free	15
Powdered, regular	Dream Whip	5 tbsp	20	½ fruit, 1 fat (S)	15
	Fluffy Whip	1 Tbsp	5	free(S)	15

ITEM	TYPE OR BRAND	MEASURE	WT. (g)	EXCHANGES	CALORIES
Nuts and Seeds					
Almonds	Any	7-8	10	1 fat (M)	45
Almond Paste	Any	½ oz	15	½ bread, 1 fat (M)	80
Brazil Nuts	Any	2 med	5	1 fat (M&P)	45
Cashews	Any	3-4	10	1 fat (M)	45
Filberts	Any	5	10	1 fat (M)	45
Hickory Nuts	Any	7-8	10	1 fat (M)	45
Macadamia Nuts	Any	6 halves, 3 whole	10	1 fat (M)	45
Mixed	Any	4-6	10	1 fat (M)	45
Peanuts	Any	8-9	10	1 fat (M)	45
Pecans	Any	5-6 halves	10	1 fat (M)	45
Pili Nuts	Any	1 tbsp	10	1 fat (S&M)	45
Pistachios	Any	20	10	1 fat (M)	45
Pumpkin Kernels	Any	1 tbsp	10	1 fat (P)	45
Sesame Seeds	Any	1 tbsp	10	1 fat (M&P)	45
Squash Kernels	Any	1 tbsp	10	1 fat (P)	45
Sunflower Kernels	Any	1 tbsp	10	1 fat (P)	45
Walnuts, Black	Any	4-5	10	1 fat (P)	45
Walnuts, English	Any	4-7	10	1 fat (P)	45
Sprouts					
Alfalfa	Any	½ cup raw	30	free	10
Mungbean	Any	½ cup raw	30	free	10
Soybean	Any	⅓ cup raw	30	free	10

II. MAIN COURSE CONVENIENCE FOODS

BEANS

ITEM	TYPE OR BRAND	MEASURE	WT. (g)	EXCHANGES	CALORIES
Baked Beans, brown sugar style	Stokely Van Camp	½ cup	130	2 bread, ½ med-fat meat	175
Barbecue or baked beans					
No pork	Canned	½ cup	120	2 bread, ½ fat	160
No pork	Homemade	½ cup	120	2½ bread, 1 low-fat meat	225
Beans & Franks in Tomato Sauce	Canned	½ cup	125	1 bread, 1 med-fat meat, ½ fat	170
Beans & Beef in Tomato Sauce	Canned	½ cup	120	1 bread, 1 med-fat meat	145
Chili Con Carne					
No Beans	Canned	1 cup	240	1 bread, 2 med-fat meat, 3 fat	355
With beans	Canned	1 cup	240	1½ bread, 2 med-fat meat, 1 fat	300
Pork & Beans, in Sauce					
Canned	Any	½ cup	120	2 bread	135
Snack Pack	Hunt's	1 can	150	2½ bread	170
Refried Beans & Sausage	Old El Paso	½ cup	100	1 bread, ½ med-fat meat, 2 fat	195
Three Bean Salad	Green Giant	⅓ cup	85	1 bread	70

ITEM	TYPE OR BRAND	MEASURE	WT. (g)	EXCHANGES	CALORIES
DELICASEAS SURIMI PRODUCTS					
Sea Pasta	Delicaseas	5 pcs	75	1½ fruit, 1 low-fat meat (Add ½ fat)*	90
Sea Stix					
Salad Style	Delicaseas	4 oz	115	1 fruit, 2 low-fat meat (add 1 fat)*	105
Whole Leg	Delicaseas	1 (4 oz)	115	1 fruit, 2 low-fat meat (add 1 fat)*	105
Sea Tails, whole	Delicaseas	1 (4 oz)	115	1 fruit, 2½ low-fat meat (add 1½ fat)*	110
GORTON'S FROZEN FISH PRODUCTS					
Breaded Fish Sticks	Gorton's	4 (3 ¼ oz)	90	1½ fruit, ½ bread, 1 med-fat meat, ½ fat	195
Crispy Batter Dipped Fish Fillets	Gorton's	4 (3 ¼ oz)	90	1 fruit, ½ bread, 1 med-fat meat, 2 fat	245
Crispy Batter Dipped Fish Sticks	Gorton's	1 (3 oz)	85	½ fruit, 1 bread, 1 med-fat meat, 1½ fat	235
Crunchy Fish Fillets	Gorton's	2 (4 oz)	115	½ veg, 1 bread, 1 med-fat meat, 4 fat	340
Crunchy Fish Sticks	Gorton's	4 (2½ oz)	70	1 bread, ½ med-fat meat, 2½ fat	220
Crunchy Fried Clam Strips	Gorton's	½ pkg (2½ oz)	70	1½ bread, ½ med-fat meat, 2½ fat	255
Fishniks 'N Chips	Gorton's	⅓ pkg (7 oz)	200	1½ veg, 3½ fruit, 1½ med-fat meat, 3 fat	430

*See EXPLANATORY NOTES for meaning of "low-fat meat" (add ½ fat.)

ITEM	TYPE OR BRAND	MEASURE	WT. (g)	EXCHANGES	CALORIES
Potato Crisp Fish Fillets	Gorton's	2 (3½ oz)	100	1 veg, 1 bread, 1 med-fat meat, 3½ fat	330
Potato Crisp Fish Sticks	Gorton's	4 (3 oz)	85	2 veg, ½ bread, ½ med-fat meat, 3½ fat	280
Value Pack Fish Sticks	Gorton's	4 (3 oz)	85	½ fruit, 1 bread, 1 med-fat meat, 1 fat	215

GORTON'S FROZEN FISH PRODUCTS-LIGHT RECIPE

ITEM	TYPE OR BRAND	MEASURE	WT. (g)	EXCHANGES	CALORIES
Baked Stuffed Scrod	Gorton's	1 pkg (6 oz)	170	1 veg, 3 med-fat meat	265
Baked Stuffed Shrimp	Gorton's	1 pkg (8 oz)	225	½ milk, 2 bread, 1 med-fat meat, 2 fat	350
Crab Au Gratin	Gorton's	1 pkg (9 oz)	255	½ milk, 1 veg, ½ bread, 2 med-fat meat, ½ fat	280
Entree Size Fish Fillet Flounder	Gorton's	1 (5 oz)	140	½ veg, ½ fruit, 1 bread, 2 med-fat meat	260
Entree Size Fish Fillet Haddock	Gorton's	1 (5 oz)	140	1½ veg, 1 bread, 2 med-fat meat	265
Filet of Haddock with Lemon Butter Sauce	Gorton's	1 pkg (6 oz)	170	½ veg, ½ fruit, 3½ low-fat meat	225
Filet of Sole with Lemon Butter Sauce	Gorton's	1 pkg (6 oz)	170	½ milk, ½ veg, 2½ med-fat meat	250
Lightly Breaded Fish Fillets	Gorton's	1 (5 oz)	140	1½ veg, ½ bread, 1 med-fat meat, ½ fat	175
Shrimp and Pasta Medley	Gorton's	1 pkg (7¼ oz)	205	1½ veg, 1½ bread, 2 med-fat meat, 1½ fat	370
Shrimp Oriental	Gorton's	1 pkg (10 oz)	285	1½ veg, 5½ fruit, ½ bread, 1 low-fat meat	350

ITEM	TYPE OR BRAND	MEASURE	WT. (g)	EXCHANGES	CALORIES
Shrimp Scampi	Gorton's	1 pkg (6⅓ oz)	180	1 veg, 1 fruit, 2½ med-fat meat, 2 fat	355
Stuffed Crabs Imperial	Gorton's	1 pkg (6⅓ oz)	180	1½ fruit, 1 bread, 2 med-fat meat, 2 fat	370
Stuffed Flounder	Gorton's	1 pkg (6½ oz)	185	1 veg, ½ bread, 2½ med-fat meat	260
Tempura Batter Fish Fillets	Gorton's	1 (3 oz)	85	1 fruit, 1½ med-fat meat, ½ fat	180
Tempura Batter Fish Sticks	Gorton's	3 (3 oz)	85	1 fruit, 1½ med-fat meat, 1 fat	205

VAN DE KAMP'S SEAFOOD ENTREES

ITEM	TYPE OR BRAND	MEASURE	WT. (g)	EXCHANGES	CALORIES
Batter-Dipped Fish & Chips	Van De Kamp's	7 oz	200	2½ bread, 2 med-fat meat, 3 fat	465
Batter-Dipped Fish Kabobs	Van De Kamp's	4 oz	115	1 bread, 1½ med-fat meat, 1½ fat	255
Batter-Dipped Fish Portions	Van De Kamp's	3 oz (2 pcs)	85	1 bread, ½ med-fat meat, 1½ fat	175
Batter-Dipped Fish Sticks	Van De Kamp's	4 oz (4 pcs)	115	1 bread, 1 med-fat meat, 1½ fat	215
Batter-Dipped Haddock	Van De Kamp's	4 oz (2 pcs)	115	1 bread, 1½ med-fat meat, ½ fat	210
Batter-Dipped Halibut	Van De Kamp's	4 oz (3 pcs)	115	1 bread, 1½ med-fat meat, 1½ fat	255
Batter-Dipped Perch	Van De Kamp's	4 oz (2 pcs)	115	1½ bread, 1½ med-fat meat, 1½ fat	290

ITEM	TYPE OR BRAND	MEASURE	WT. (g)	EXCHANGES	CALORIES
Batter-Dipped Sole	Van De Kamp's	4 oz (2 pcs)	115	1½ bread, 1½ med-fat meat, 1 fat	265
Country Seasoned Fish Fillets	Van De Kamp's	2 cz (1 pc)	55	1 bread, ½ med-fat meat, 2 fat	200
Light & Crispy Fish Fillets	Van De Kamp's	2 oz (1 pc)	55	½ bread, ½ med-fat meat, 2 fat	165
Light & Cripsy Fish Nuggets	Van De Kamp's	2 oz	55	½ bread, 1 med-fat meat, ½ fat	135
Light & Crispy Fish Sticks	Van De Kamp's	3¾ oz (4 pcs)	105	1 bread, 1 med-fat meat, 2½ fat	260
Light & Crispy Haddock Fillets	Van De Kamp's	2 oz (1 pc)	55	½ bread, ½ med-fat meat, 2 fat	165
Light & Crispy Perch Fillets	Van De Kamp's	2 oz (1 pc)	55	½ bread, ½ med-fat meat, 2 fat	165
Lightly Breaded Cod	Van De Kamp's	5 oz (1 pc)	140	1 bread, 2 med-fat meat, 1½ fat	290
Lightly Breaded Flounder	Van De Kamp's	5 oz (1 pc)	140	1 bread, 2 med-fat meat, 1½ fat	295
Lightly Breaded Sole	Van De Kamp's	5 oz (1 pc)	140	1 bread, 2 med-fat meat, 1½ fat	295

ITEM	TYPE OR BRAND	MEASURE	WT. (g)	EXCHANGES	CALORIES
BIRDS EYE INTERNATIONAL RICE RECIPES (frozen)					
Chinese Fried Style	Birds Eye	⅓ pkg (3⅗ oz)	100	1½ bread	105
French Style	Birds Eye	⅓ pkg (3⅗ oz)	100	½ fruit, 1½ bread	125
Italian Style	Birds Eye	⅓ pkg (3⅗ oz)	100	½ fruit, 1½ bread	125
Spanish Style	Birds Eye	⅓ pkg (3⅗ oz)	100	½ fruit, 1½ bread	125
CHICKEN HELPER					
Chicken and Dumpling	Betty Crocker	⅕ pkg*	var	2 veg, 2 bread, 3½ med-fat meat, 1½ fat	530
Chicken and Mushroom	Betty Crocker	⅕ pkg*	var	3½ veg, 1½ fruit, 3½ med-fat meat, 1 fat	470
Potato and Gravy	Betty Crocker	⅕ pkg*	var	4½ veg, 1½ fruit, ½ bread, 3½ med-fat meat, 2½ fat	600
Stuffing	Betty Crocker	⅕ pkg*	var	2 veg, ½ fruit, 1½ bread, 4 med-fat meat, 2 fat	585
Teriyaki Chicken	Betty Crocker	⅕ pkg*	var	2 veg, 3 fruit, 4 med-fat meat, ½ fat	510
FRANCO AMERICAN CANNED PRODUCTS					
Beef Ravioli in Meat Sauce	Franco American	7½ oz	215	3 veg, 1½ bread, 1 fat	225
Beef RavioliOs in Meat Sauce	Franco American	7½ oz	215	2½ veg, 1½ bread, 1 fat	210
BeefyOs and Beef in Tomato Sauce	Franco American	7½ oz	215	2 bread, ½ med-fat meat, 1 fat	225

*Prepared according to package directions with 3 lb. chicken and other ingredients.

ITEM	TYPE OR BRAND	MEASURE	WT. (g)	EXCHANGES	CALORIES
Elbow Macaroni and Cheese	Franco American	7⅜ oz	210	½ milk, 1 bread, 1 fat	155
Macaroni and Cheese	Franco American	7⅜ oz	210	½ milk, 1 bread, 1 fat	155
PizzOs in Zesty Pizza Sauce	Franco American	7½ oz	215	1 veg, ½ fruit, 1½ bread, ½ fat	170
Spaghetti in Meat Sauce	Franco American	7½ oz	215	½ veg, 1½ bread, ½ med-fat meat, 1 fat	200
Spaghetti in Tomato Sauce with Cheese	Franco American	7⅜ oz	210	1 veg, 1 fruit, 1½ bread, ½ fat	190
Spaghetti with Meatballs in Tomato Sauce	Franco American	7⅜ oz	210	1 fruit, 1 bread, 1 med-fat meat, ½ fat	210
"SpaghettiOs" in Tomato and Cheese Sauce	Franco American	7⅜ oz	210	½ veg, 1 fruit, 1½ bread, ½ fat	180
"SpaghettiOs" with Meatballs in Tomato Sauce	Franco American	7⅜ oz	210	1 fruit, 1 bread, 1 med-fat meat, ½ fat	210
"SpaghettiOs" with Sliced Beef Franks in Tomato Sauce	Franco American	7⅜ oz	210	1 fruit, 1 bread, ½ med-fat meat, 1½ fat	215
UFOs	Franco American	7½ oz	215	½ veg, 2 bread, ½ fat	175
UFOs with Meteors (meatballs)	Franco American	7½ oz	215	2 bread, ½ med-fat meat, 1 fat	225

GREEN GIANT RICE ORIGINALS (frozen)

ITEM	TYPE OR BRAND	MEASURE	WT. (g)	EXCHANGES	CALORIES
Italian Blend White Rice & Spinach in Cheese Sauce	Green Giant	½ cup	75	1 veg, 1 bread, 1½ fat	160
Long Grain White & Wild Rice	Green Giant	½ cup	75	1½ bread, ½ fat	125
Rice Medley	Green Giant	½ cup	75	1½ bread, ½ fat	125

ITEM	TYPE OR BRAND	MEASURE	WT. (g)	EXCHANGES	CALORIES
Rice 'n Broccoli in Flavored Cheese Sauce	Green Giant	½ cup	75	½ veg, 1 bread, 1 fat	125
Rice Pilaf	Green Giant	½ cup	75	1½ bread, ½ fat	125
Rice with Herb Butter Sauce	Green Giant	½ cup	75	1½ bread, 1 fat	150
HAMBURGER HELPER					
Beef Noodle	Betty Crocker	⅕ pkg*	var	2 veg, 1 bread, 2 med-fat meat, 1 fat	325
Beef Romanoff	Betty Crocker	⅕ pkg*	var	2½ veg, 1 bread, 2 med-fat meat, 1 fat	335
Cheeseburger Macaroni	Betty Crocker	⅕ pkg*	var	2½ veg, 1 bread, 2 med-fat meat, 1½ fat	360
Chili Tomato	Betty Crocker	⅕ pkg*	var	½ veg, 3 fruit, 2½ med-fat meat	330
Hamburger Hash	Betty Crocker	⅕ pkg*	var	½ veg, 1½ bread, 2 med-fat meat, 1 fat	320
Hamburger Pizza Dish	Betty Crocker	⅕ pkg*	var	½ veg, 1½ fruit, 1 bread, 2½ med-fat meat	340
Hamburger Stew	Betty Crocker	⅕ pkg*	var	2½ veg, 1 fruit, 2 med-fat meat, ½ fat	285
Lasagne	Betty Crocker	⅕ pkg*	var	½ milk, 1½ fruit, ½ bread, 2 med-fat meat, ½ fat	315
Pizzabake	Betty Crocker	⅙ pkg*	var	1 veg, 2½ fruit, 2½ med-fat meat	325

*Prepared according to package directions with 1 lb. ground beef.

PASTA AND RICE PRODUCTS

ITEM	TYPE OR BRAND	MEASURE	WT. (g)	EXCHANGES	CALORIES
Potatoes Au Gratin	Betty Crocker	⅕ pkg*	var	1 milk, 1 bread, 1 med-fat meat, 2 fat	320
Potatoes Stroganoff	Betty Crocker	⅕ pkg*	var	1 milk, 1 bread, 1 med-fat meat, 2 fat	320
Rice Oriental	Betty Crocker	⅕ pkg*	var	½ fruit, 2 bread, 2 med-fat meat, ½ fat	340
Spaghetti	Betty Crocker	⅕ pkg*	var	1½ fruit, 1 bread, 2½ med-fat meat	330
Tamale Pie	Betty Crocker	⅕ pkg*	var	2½ bread, 2 med-fat meat, 1 fat	380

INTERNATIONAL NOODLE MIXES

ITEM	TYPE OR BRAND	MEASURE	WT. (g)	EXCHANGES	CALORIES
Fettuccine Alfredo	Betty Crocker	¼ pkg**	var	1½ bread, ½ med-fat meat, 1½ fat	210
Parisienne	Betty Crocker	¼ pkg**	var	½ milk, ½ fruit, 1 bread, 1 fat	175
Romanoff	Betty Crocker	¼ pkg**	var	½ milk, ½ veg, 1 bread, 2½ fat	235
Stroganoff	Betty Crocker	¼ pkg**	var	½ milk, ½ veg, 1 bread, 2½ fat	235

*Prepared according to package directions with 1 lb. ground beef.

**Prepared according to package directions.

ITEM	TYPE OR BRAND	MEASURE	WT. (g)	EXCHANGES	CALORIES
KRAFT DINNERS					
American Style Spaghetti	Kraft	1 cup*	225	1½ fruit, 2 bread, ½ med-fat meat, 1 fat	280
Egg Noodle and Cheese	Kraft	⅔ cup*	150	½ milk, ½ fruit, 1 bread, 3 fat	265
Egg Noodle with Chicken	Kraft	¾ cup*	170	½ milk, ½ veg, 1½ bread, 2 fat	245
Macaroni and Cheese	Kraft	¾ cup*	170	½ milk, 2 bread, 3 fat	315
Macaroni and Cheese-Family Style	Kraft	¾ cup*	170	½ milk, 2 bread, 3 fat	315
Macaroni and Cheese Deluxe	Kraft	¾ cup*	170	½ milk, 2 bread, ½ med-fat meat, 1 fat	265
Spaghetti with Meat Sauce	Kraft	¾ cup*	170	1½ fruit, 1 bread, 1 med-fat meat, 1 fat	255
Spiral Macaroni and Cheese	Kraft	¾ cup*	170	1 milk, ½ fruit, 1 bread, 3 fat	305
Tangy Italian Style Spaghetti	Kraft	1 cup*	225	2 fruit, 1½ bread, 1 med-fat meat, ½ fat	285
TUNA HELPER					
Au Gratin	Betty Crocker	⅕ pkg**	var	½ milk, 1½ veg, 1 bread, 1 med-fat meat, 1½ fat	295
Cold Salad	Betty Crocker	⅕ pkg**	var	½ milk, 1½ bread, 1 med-fat meat, 5 fat	450

*Prepared according to package directions.

**Prepared according to package directions with 6½ oz. canned tuna and other ingredients.

ITEM	TYPE OR BRAND	MEASURE	WT. (g)	EXCHANGES	CALORIES
Country Dumplings, Noodles 'n Tuna	Betty Crocker	⅕ pkg*	var	1½ veg, 1½ bread, 1 med-fat meat, 1 fat	265
Creamy Noodles 'n Tuna	Betty Crocker	⅕ pkg*	var	1½ veg, 1½ bread, 1 med-fat meat, 1 fat	265
Noodles, Cheese Sauce 'n Tuna	Betty Crocker	⅕ pkg*	var	½ milk, 1½ bread, 1 med-fat meat, ½ fat	245
Tuna Tetrazzini	Betty Crocker	⅕ pkg*	var	½ veg, 1½ bread, 1½ med-fat meat, ½ fat	260

*Prepared according to package directions with 6½ oz. canned tuna and other ingredients.

NOTE: There is much variation among different frozen pizzas in both ingredients and serving sizes. Many frozen pizzas are high fat items containing as much as 50% of total calories from fat. Read the label carefully.

ITEM	TYPE OR BRAND	MEASURE	WT. (g)	EXCHANGES	CALORIES
CELESTE FROZEN PIZZA					
Canadian Style Bacon Pizza	Celeste (Quaker)	¼ pizza	135	½ veg, 1 fruit, 1 bread, 2 med-fat meat, 1 fat	325
Cheese Pizza	Celeste (Quaker)	¼ pizza	125	½ milk, 1½ bread, 1 med-fat meat, 2 fat	315
Deluxe Pizza	Celeste (Quaker)	¼ pizza	160	3 veg, 1 bread, 1 med-fat meat, 3½ fat	380
Pepperoni Pizza	Celeste (Quaker)	¼ pizza	135	3 veg, 1 bread, 1 med-fat meat, 3 fat	360
Sausage Pizza	Celeste (Quaker)	¼ pizza	140	1½ fruit, 1 bread, 2 med-fat meat, 2 fat	380
Sausage and Mushroom Pizza	Celeste (Quaker)	¼ pizza	175	½ milk, 1 fruit, 1 bread, 1½ med-fat meat, 3 fat	400
Suprema Pizza	Celeste (Quaker)	¼ pizza	165	½ milk, 1 fruit, 1 bread, 1½ med-fat meat, 3 fat	400
CELESTE SINGLE SERVING FROZEN PIZZA					
Canadian Style Bacon Pizza	Celeste (Quaker)	1 pizza (7¾ oz)	220	2½ veg, 2½ bread, 2½ med-fat meat, 2½ fat	550
Cheese Pizza	Celeste (Quaker)	1 pizza (6½ oz)	185	½ milk, 2 fruit, 1½ bread, 2 med-fat meat, 2½ fat	495
Deluxe Pizza	Celeste (Quaker)	1 pizza (8¼ oz)	235	½ milk, 1½ veg, 2½ bread, 1½ med-fat meat, 4½ fat	575

PIZZA

ITEM	TYPE OR BRAND	MEASURE	WT. (g)	EXCHANGES	CALORIES
Pepperoni Pizza	Celeste (Quaker)	1 pizza (6¾ oz)	190	1 milk, 3 veg, 1½ bread, ½ med-fat meat, 5½ fat	545
Sausage Pizza	Celeste (Quaker)	1 pizza (7½ oz)	215	1 veg, 2 fruit, 1½ bread, 2½ med-fat meat, 3½ fat	565
Sausage and Mushroom Pizza	Celeste (Quaker)	1 pizza (8½ oz)	240	1½ milk, ½ veg, 2 bread, 1 med-fat meat, 5½ fat	600
Suprema Pizza	Celeste (Quaker)	1 pizza (9 oz)	255	½ milk, 1 fruit, 2½ bread, 2½ med-fat meat, 5 fat	680

TOTINO'S EXTRA! CRISP CRUST PIZZA

ITEM	TYPE OR BRAND	MEASURE	WT. (g)	EXCHANGES	CALORIES
Combination Sausage & Pepperoni Pizza	Pillsbury	¼ pizza (10″ dia)	100	½ milk, 1 veg, 1 bread, ½ med-fat meat, 2½ fat	285
Pepperoni Pizza	Pillsbury	¼ pizza (10″ dia)	95	½ milk, ½ veg, 1 bread, ½ med-fat meat, 2 fat	250
Sausage Pizza	Pillsbury	¼ pizza (10″ dia)	100	½ milk, ½ veg, 1 bread, ½ med-fat meat, 2½ fat	275

TOTINO'S HEAT 'n EAT MICROWAVE PIZZA

ITEM	TYPE OR BRAND	MEASURE	WT. (g)	EXCHANGES	CALORIES
Cheese Pizza	Pillsbury	1 pizza (5½″ dia)	115	1 milk, 1 veg, 1 bread, 2 fat	265
Combination Sausage and Pepperoni Pizza	Pillsbury	1 pizza (5½″ dia)	140	½ milk, ½ veg, 2 bread, 1 med-fat meat, 3 fat	370
Pepperoni Pizza	Pillsbury	1 pizza (5½″ dia)	130	½ milk, 1 fruit, 1 bread, 1 med-fat meat, 2½ fat	340
Sausage Pizza	Pillsbury	1 pizza (5½″ dia)	135	½ milk, 1 fruit, 1 bread, 1 med-fat meat, 3 fat	365

ITEM	TYPE OR BRAND	MEASURE	WT. (g)	EXCHANGES	CALORIES
TOTINO'S MY CLASSIC PIZZA					
Canadian Style Bacon Pizza	Pillsbury	¼ pizza (11½" dia)	145	½ milk, 1 fruit, 1½ bread, 1½ med-fat meat, ½ fat	325
Cheese Pizza	Pillsbury	¼ pizza (11½" dia)	135	1½ milk, 1½ bread, 3 fat	360
Combination Sausage and Pepperoni Pizza	Pillsbury	¼ pizza (11½" dia)	165	½ milk, ½ fruit, 2 bread, 5 fat	420
Pepperoni Pizza	Pillsbury	¼ pizza (11½" dia)	150	1 milk, ½ fruit, 1½ bread, 3 fat	415
Sausage Pizza	Pillsbury	¼ pizza (11½" dia)	165	½ milk, ½ fruit, 1½ bread, 1 med-fat meat, 3 fat	450
TOTINO'S PARTY CRISP CRUST FROZEN PIZZA					
Canadian Style Bacon Pizza	Pillsbury	⅓ pizza (9¼" dia)	105	½ milk, ½ fruit, 1 bread, ½ med-fat meat, 1½ fat	235
Combination Sausage & Pepperoni Pizza	Pillsbury	⅓ pizza (9¼" dia)	105	½ milk, ½ fruit, 1 bread, ½ med-fat meat, 2 fat	260
Cheese Pizza	Pillsbury	⅓ pizza (9¼" dia)	100	1 milk, 1 bread, 2 fat	240
Hamburger Pizza	Pillsbury	⅓ pizza (9¼" dia)	105	½ milk, 1 veg, 1 bread, ½ med-fat meat, 2 fat	265
Mexican Style Pizza	Pillsbury	⅓ pizza (9¼" dia)	90	½ milk, 1 bread, 3 fat	245
Nacho Style Pizza	Pillsbury	⅓ pizza (9¼" dia)	90	½ milk, 1 bread, ½ med-fat meat, 2 fat	240
Pepperoni	Pillsbury	⅓ pizza (9¼" dia)	105	½ milk, 1½ veg, 2½ fat	260
Sausage	Pillsbury	⅓ pizza (9¼" dia)	105	½ milk, 1½ veg, 1 bread, 2½ fat	260

POTATOES

ITEM	TYPE OR BRAND	MEASURE	WT. (g)	EXCHANGES	CALORIES
Au Gratin (with cheese)	Homemade	½ cup	100	1 bread, ½ med-fat meat, 1 fat	150

BETTY CROCKER DRY POTATO MIXES

Au Gratin	Betty Crocker	⅙ pkg*	var	1½ bread, 1 fat	150
Chicken 'n Herb	Betty Crocker	⅙ pkg*	var	½ veg, 1 bread, 1 fat	125
Creamed	Betty Crocker	⅙ pkg*	var	½ veg, 1½ bread, 1½ fat	185
Hash Browns with Onions	Betty Crocker	⅙ pkg*	var	½ fruit, 1 bread, 1 fat	135
Hickory Smoke Cheese	Betty Crocker	⅙ pkg*	var	1½ bread, 1 fat	150
Julienne	Betty Crocker	⅙ pkg*	var	½ veg, 1 bread, 1 fat	125
Potato Buds	Betty Crocker	⅙ pkg*	var	½ veg, 1 bread, 1 fat	125
Scalloped	Betty Crocker	⅙ pkg*	var	½ veg, 1 bread, 1 fat	125
Sour Cream 'n Chive	Betty Crocker	⅙ pkg*	var	1½ bread, 1½ fat	170
French Fries	Any	8 pcs (½x½x2″)	40	1 bread, 1 fat	115
Fried	Homemade	½ cup	85	2 bread, 2 fat	180

GREEN GIANT POTATO ORIGINALS

Stuffed Baked Potato with Cheese Flavored Topping	Green Giant	½ pkg (5 oz)	140	½ fruit, 2 bread, 1 fat	205
Stuffed Baked Potato with Sour Cream & Chives	Green Giant	½ pkg (5 oz)	140	½ veg, 2 bread, 2 fat	240
Hash Browns	Homemade or frozen	½ cup	100	1 bread, 1 fat	115
Mashed, with fat added	Instant or homemade	½ cup	100	1 bread, 1 fat	115

*Prepared according to package directions.

ITEM	TYPE OR BRAND	MEASURE	WT. (g)	EXCHANGES	CALORIES
Potato Puffs	Birds Eye	½ cup	100	1 bread, 2 fat	160
Potato Salad					
Mayonnaise, eggs	Homemade	½ cup	100	1 bread, 2 fat	160
Salad dressing, eggs	Homemade	½ cup	100	1 bread, 1 fat	115
Scalloped	Homemade or frozen	½ cup	100	1 bread, 1 fat	115
Tater Tots, frozen	Any	½ cup	100	1 bread, 1½ fat	135

POTPIES AND STEWS

ITEM	TYPE OR BRAND	MEASURE	WT. (g)	EXCHANGES	CALORIES
BANQUET MEAT PIES					
Beef	Banquet	1 pie (8 oz)	225	2 veg, 2½ bread, 1 med-fat meat, 5½ fat	550
Chicken	Banquet	1 pie (8 oz)	225	3 veg, 2 bread, 1 med-fat meat, 5 fat	520
Tuna	Banquet	1 pie (8 oz)	225	1½ veg, 1 fruit, 2 bread, 1½ med-fat meat, 4 fat	515
Turkey	Banquet	1 pie (8 oz)	225	2 veg, 2 bread, 1½ med-fat meat, 5 fat	530
Beef Potpie, homemade	1 crust*	⅙ (9″ pie)	var	1 veg, 2 bread, 3 med-fat meat, 2 fat	485
	2 crust*	⅙ (9″ pie)	var	1 veg, 2½ bread, 3 med-fat meat, 3 fat	565
Beef Stew	Canned	1 cup (½ can)	240	1 veg, 1 bread, 1 med-fat meat, ½ fat	195
	Homemade**	⅙ recipe	var	1 veg, 1 bread, 3 med-fat meat, ½ fat	350
Chicken a la King	Swanson	7⅝ oz	215	1 veg, ½ fruit, 1 med-fat meat, 1½ fat	190
Chicken & Dumplings	Swanson	5¼ oz	150	1 veg, 1 bread, 1 med-fat meat, 1½ fat	240
Chicken Stew	Swanson	7½ oz	215	1 bread, 1 med-fat meat, ½ fat	170

*Standard pastry recipe used for one or two-crust beef pies.

**Stew recipe (serves 6): 24 oz stew meat (18 oz ckd), 1 tbsp flour, 1 tbsp oil, ½ cup onion, 6 small carrots, 6 small potatoes.

ITEM	TYPE OR BRAND	MEASURE	WT. (g)	EXCHANGES	CALORIES
SWANSON CHUNKY PIES					
Chunky Beef	Swanson	1 pie (10 oz)	285	1 veg, 3½ bread, 1½ med-fat meat, 4½ fat	590
Chunky Chicken	Swanson	1 pie (10 oz)	285	1 veg, 3½ bread, 1½ med-fat meat, 4½ fat	590
Chunky Turkey	Swanson	1 pie (10 oz)	285	3½ veg, 2 bread, 1 med-fat meat, 5 fat	530
SWANSON HUNGRY-MAN MEAT PIES					
Hungry-Man Beef	Swanson	1 pie (16 oz)	455	5½ veg, 2½ bread, 1½ med-fat meat, 5½ fat	675
Hungry-Man Chicken	Swanson	1 pie (16 oz)	455	5 veg, 2½ bread, 2 med-fat meat, 6 fat	735
Hungry-Man Steak Burger	Swanson	1 pie (16 oz)	455	5½ veg, 2½ bread, 2 med-fat meat, 7½ fat	810
Hungry-Man Turkey	Swanson	1 pie (16 oz)	455	5 veg, 2½ bread, 2 med-fat meat, 6 fat	735
SWANSON MEAT PIES					
Beef	Swanson	1 pie (8 oz)	225	½ veg, 2½ bread, 1 med-fat meat, 3½ fat	425
Chicken	Swanson	1 pie (8 oz)	225	½ veg, 2½ bread, 1 med-fat meat, 3½ fat	425
Macaroni and Cheese	Swanson	1 pie (7 oz)	200	1 milk, ½ fruit, ½ bread, 2 fat	225
Turkey	Swanson	1 pie (8 oz)	225	2 veg, 2 bread, ½ med-fat meat, 4½ fat	430

NOTE: Exchanges for mixes are calculated for the product prepared according to package directions.

ITEM	TYPE OR BRAND	MEASURE	WT. (g)	EXCHANGES	CALORIES
Barbecue Sauce	Bottled	2 tbsp	25	½ fruit	20
Catsup	Any	1½ tbsp max	20	½ fruit	20
◆ Chocolate Flavored Syrup	Hershey	1½ tbsp	20	1 bread	70
◆ Chocolate Fudge Topping	Hershey	2 tbsp	25	1½ fruit, 1 fat	105
Chili Sauce	Bottled	1½ tbsp	20	½ fruit	20
Gravy					
Beef	Canned	¼ cup	70	½ med-fat meat	40
Brown, thick	Homemade	¼ cup	75	½ bread, 3 fat	170
Brown	Mix	¼ cup max	70	free	5
Chicken	Canned	¼ cup	70	½ veg, 1 fat	60
Chicken	Mix	¼ cup	70	½ fruit	20
Mushroom	Canned	¼ cup	70	½ veg, ½ fat	35
Mushroom	Mix	¼ cup	70	½ veg	15
Onion	Mix	¼ cup	70	½ veg	15
Pork	Mix	¼ cup	70	½ veg	15
Turkey	Canned	¼ cup	70	½ fruit, ½ low-fat meat	45
Turkey	Mix	¼ cup	70	½ veg	15
Hollandaise Sauce	Homemade	¼ cup	70	½ med-fat meat, 3 fat	175
	Mix	¼ cup	70	½ bread, 2 fat	125
Horseradish	Any	1 tbsp	20	free	5

ITEM	TYPE OR BRAND	MEASURE	WT. (g)	EXCHANGES	CALORIES
KRAFT TOPPINGS					
◆ Caramel	Kraft	1½ tbsp	25	1 bread	70
◆ Chocolate Flavored	Kraft	1½ tbsp	25	1 bread	70
◆ Fudge	Kraft	1 tbsp	20	1 fruit, ½ fat	60
◆ Pineapple	Kraft	1½ tbsp	25	2 fruit	80
◆ Strawberry	Kraft	1 tbsp	20	1 fruit	40
◆ Walnut	Kraft	1 tbsp	20	1 fruit, 1 fat	95
Mushroom Sauce	Mix	¼ cup	70	1½ veg, ½ fat	65
Picante Sauce	Bottled	6 tbsp	85	½ bread	35
Sour Cream Sauce	Mix	¼ cup	70	1 veg, 1½ fat	95
Soy Sauce	Any	2 tbsp max	30	free	15
Spaghetti Sauce Mix	Any	⅙ pkg	40	free	15
◆ Sweet and Sour Sauce	Bottled	2 tbsp	35	1½ fruit	60
Taco Sauce	Any	1 tbsp max	15	free	10
Tartar Sauce	Bottled	1 tbsp	20	2 fat	90
Teriyaki Sauce	Bottled	1 tbsp max	15	free	15
Tobasco Sauce	Any	1 tsp	5	free	5
Tomato Paste	Any	6 oz can	180	4 veg, 1 fruit	150

ITEM	TYPE OR BRAND	MEASURE	WT. (g)	EXCHANGES	CALORIES
Tomato Sauce	Any	8 oz can	240	2 veg, ½ fruit	75
White Sauce, medium, non-fat milk	Homemade or mix	¼ cup	70	½ bread, 1 fat	80
	Homemade or mix	1¼ cup	350	1 bread, 1 milk, 6 fat	420
White Sauce, medium, whole milk	Homemade or mix	¼ cup	70	½ bread, 1½ fat	100
	Homemade or mix	1¼ cup	350	1 bread, 1 milk, 8 fat	510
Worchestershire Sauce	Bottled	1 tbsp max	15	free	15

ITEM	TYPE OR BRAND	MEASURE	WT. (g)	EXCHANGES	CALORIES
CAMPBELL SOUPS					
Asparagus, Cream of	Campbell	1 cup (8 oz)*	225	½ veg, ½ bread, 1 fat	90
Bean with Bacon	Campbell	1 cup (8 oz)*	225	1½ bread, ½ med-fat meat, ½ fat	165
Beef	Campbell	1 cup (8 oz)*	225	½ veg, ½ bread, ½ med-fat meat	85
Beef Broth (Bouillon)	Campbell	1 cup (8 oz)*	225	½ low-fat meat	30
Beef Noodle	Campbell	1 cup (8 oz)*	225	½ bread, ½ med-fat meat	75
Beef Noodle, Homestyle	Campbell	1 cup (8 oz)*	225	½ bread, ½ med-fat meat	75
Beefy Mushroom	Campbell	1 cup (8 oz)*	225	1 veg, ½ med-fat meat	65
Black Bean	Campbell	1 cup (8 oz)*	225	2 veg, ½ bread, ½ fat	105
Celery, Cream of	Campbell	1 cup (8 oz)*	225	½ bread, 1½ fat	100
Cheddar Cheese	Campbell	1 cup (8 oz)*	225	½ milk, 1½ fat	105
Chicken Alphabet	Campbell	1 cup (8 oz)*	225	½ bread, ½ med-fat meat	75
Chicken Broth	Campbell	1 cup (8 oz)*	225	½ low-fat meat	30
Chicken Broth and Noodles	Campbell	1 cup (8 oz)*	225	½ bread, ½ fat	55
Chicken Broth and Rice	Campbell	1 cup (8 oz)*	225	½ bread	35
Chicken and Stars	Campbell	1 cup (8 oz)*	225	1½ veg, ½ fat	60
Chicken, Cream of	Campbell	1 cup (8 oz)*	225	½ milk, 1½ fat	105

*4 oz. canned soup + 4 oz. water.

SOUPS

ITEM	TYPE OR BRAND	MEASURE	WT. (g)	EXCHANGES	CALORIES
Chicken Gumbo	Campbell	1 cup (8 oz)*	225	½ veg, ½ bread, ½ fat	70
Chicken 'n Dumplings	Campbell	1 cup (8 oz)*	225	½ bread, ½ med-fat meat	75
Chicken Noodle	Campbell	1 cup (8 oz)*	225	½ bread, ½ med-fat meat	75
Chicken Noodle, Homestyle	Campbell	1 cup (8 oz)*	225	½ bread, ½ med-fat meat	75
Chicken Noodle O's	Campbell	1 cup (8 oz)*	225	½ veg, ½ bread, ½ fat	70
Chicken Vegetable	Campbell	1 cup (8 oz)*	225	1½ veg, ½ fat	60
Chicken with Rice	Campbell	1 cup (8 oz)*	225	½ bread, ½ fat	55
Chili Beef	Campbell	1 cup (8 oz)*	225	1 bread, ½ med-fat meat, ½ fat	130
Clam Chowder, Manhattan Style	Campbell	1 cup (8 oz)*	225	½ veg, ½ bread, ½ fat	70
Clam Chowder, New England	Campbell	1 cup (8 oz)*	225	1 veg, ½ bread, ½ fat	80
Consommé (Beef) Gelatin Added	Campbell	1 cup (8 oz)*	225	½ low-fat meat	25
Creamy Chicken Mushroom	Campbell	1 cup (8 oz)*	225	½ milk, 1½ fat	105
Curly Noodle with Chicken	Campbell	1 cup (8 oz)*	225	½ bread, ½ med-fat meat	75
French Onion	Campbell	1 cup (8 oz)*	225	½ veg, ½ bread, ½ fat	70
Green Pea	Campbell	1 cup (8 oz)*	225	½ veg, 1½ bread, ½ med-fat meat	155
Meatball Alphabet	Campbell	1 cup (8 oz)*	225	½ veg, ½ bread, ½ med-fat meat	85
Minestrone	Campbell	1 cup (8 oz)*	225	1 veg, ½ bread, ½ fat	80

*4 oz. canned soup + 4 oz. water.

ITEM	TYPE OR BRAND	MEASURE	WT. (g)	EXCHANGES	CALORIES
Mushroom, Cream of	Campbell	1 cup (8 oz)*	225	½ bread, 1½ fat	100
Mushroom, Golden	Campbell	1 cup (8 oz)*	225	½ veg, ½ bread, ½ fat	70
Noodles and Ground Beef	Campbell	1 cup (8 oz)*	225	½ veg, ½ bread, ½ med-fat meat	85
Onion, Cream of	Campbell	1 cup (8 oz)*	225	1 veg, ½ bread, 1 fat	105
Oyster Stew	Campbell	1 cup (8 oz)*	225	½ milk, 1 fat	85
Pepperpot	Campbell	1 cup (8 oz)*	225	½ veg, ½ bread, ½ med-fat meat	85
Potato, Cream of	Campbell	1 cup (8 oz)*	225	½ veg, ½ bread, ½ fat	70
Scotch Broth	Campbell	1 cup (8 oz)*	225	2 veg, ½ fat	70
Shrimp, Cream of	Campbell	1 cup (8 oz)*	225	½ veg, ½ bread, 1 fat	90
Spanish Style Vegetable (Gazpacho)	Campbell	1 cup (8 oz)*	225	1 fruit	40
Split Pea with Ham & Bacon	Campbell	1 cup (8 oz)*	225	3½ veg, ½ bread, 1 fat	165
Tomato	Campbell	1 cup (8 oz)*	225	½ veg, 1½ fruit, ½ fat	95
Tomato, Bisque of	Campbell	1 cup (8 oz)*	225	½ veg, 2 fruit, ½ fat	115
Tomato Rice, Old Fashioned	Campbell	1 cup (8 oz)*	225	1½ fruit, ½ bread, ½ fat	120
Turkey Noodle	Campbell	1 cup (8 oz)*	225	½ veg, ½ bread, ½ fat	70
Turkey Vegetable	Campbell	1 cup (8 oz)*	225	½ veg, ½ bread, ½ fat	70
Vegetable	Campbell	1 cup (8 oz)*	225	½ veg, ½ bread, ½ fat	70

*4 oz. canned soup + 4 oz. water.

SOUPS

ITEM	TYPE OR BRAND	MEASURE	WT. (g)	EXCHANGES	CALORIES
Vegetable Beef	Campbell	1 cup (8 oz)*	225	2 veg, ½ fat	70
Vegetable, Old Fashioned	Campbell	1 cup (8 oz)*	225	½ veg, ½ bread, ½ fat	70
Vegetarian Vegetable	Campbell	1 cup (8 oz)*	225	½ veg, ½ fruit, ½ fat	55
Won Ton	Campbell	1 cup (8 oz)*	225	½ fruit, ½ low-fat meat	45
CAMPBELL SOUPS FOR ONE (Semi-condensed)					
Burly Vegetable Beef and Bacon	Campbell	1 can (11 oz)**	310	4 veg, 1 fat	145
Clam Chowder, New England	Campbell	1 can (11 oz)**	310	2 veg, ½ bread, 1 fat	130
Full Flavored Chicken Vegetable	Campbell	1 can (11 oz)**	310	1½ veg, ½ bread, 1 fat	115
Golden Chicken and Noodles	Campbell	1 can (11 oz)**	310	1 bread, ½ med-fat meat	110
Old Fashioned Bean with Ham	Campbell	1 can (11 oz)**	310	3 veg, 1 bread, 1½ fat	210
Savory Cream of Mushroom	Campbell	1 can (11 oz)**	310	1 veg, ½ bread, 2½ fat	170
Tomato Royale	Campbell	1 can (11 oz)**	310	1½ veg, 3 fruit, ½ fat	180
Vegetable, Old World	Campbell	1 can (11 oz)**	310	2 veg, 1 fruit, 1 fat	135
CAMPBELL CHUNKY SOUPS (19 oz. size) NOTE: Use as it comes from the can (undiluted).					
Chunky Beef	Campbell	½ can (9½ oz)	270	2½ veg, ½ bread, 1 med-fat meat	175
Chunky Chicken Noodle	Campbell	½ can (9½ oz)	270	2 veg, ½ bread, 1 med-fat meat, ½ fat	185
Chunky Chicken Rice	Campbell	½ can (9½ oz)	270	1½ veg, ½ bread, 1 med-fat meat	150

*4 oz. canned soup + 4 oz. water.

**7¾ oz. canned soup + 3¼ oz. water.

ITEM	TYPE OR BRAND	MEASURE	WT. (g)	EXCHANGES	CALORIES
Chunky Chicken Vegetable	Campbell	½ can (9½ oz)	270	1 veg, 1 bread, 1 med-fat meat	175
Chunky Chili Beef	Campbell	½ can (9¾ oz)	275	½ veg, 2 bread, 2 low-fat meat	260
Chunky Clam Chowder, Manhattan Style	Campbell	½ can (9½ oz)	270	1½ veg, 1½ fruit, ½ med-fat meat	135
Chunky Clam Chowder, New England Style	Campbell	½ can (9½ oz)	270	½ milk, 2 veg, ½ fruit, 3 fat	245
Chunky Mediterranean Vegetable	Campbell	½ can (9½ oz)	270	1½ veg, 1 bread, 1 fat	150
Chunky Minestrone	Campbell	½ can (9½ oz)	270	2 veg, 1 fruit, 1 fat	135
Chunky Old Fashioned Bean with Ham	Campbell	½ can (9⅝ oz)	275	½ veg, 2 bread, 1 med-fat meat, ½ fat	255
Chunky Old Fashioned Chicken	Campbell	½ can (9½ oz)	270	3½ veg, 1 med-fat meat, ½ fat	150
Chunky Old Fashioned Vegetable Beef	Campbell	½ can (9½ oz)	270	3½ veg, ½ med-fat meat, ½ fat	150
Chunky Sirloin Burger	Campbell	½ can (9½ oz)	270	1 veg, 1 bread, 1 med-fat meat, ½ fat	195
Chunky Split Pea 'n Ham	Campbell	½ can (9½ oz)	270	3 veg, I bread, ½ med-fat meat, ½ fat	205
Chunky Steak 'n Potato	Campbell	½ can (9½ oz)	270	4 veg, ½ med-fat meat, ½ fat	165
Chunky Turkey Vegetable	Campbell	½ can (9⅜ oz)	265	3 veg, ½ med-fat meat, ½ fat	135
Chunky Vegetable	Campbell	½ can (9½ oz)	270	1½ veg, 1 fruit, 1 fat	120

SOUPS DRIED

ITEM	TYPE OR BRAND	MEASURE	WT. (g)	EXCHANGES	CALORIES
LIPTON DRIED SOUPS					
Beef Flavor Mushroom	Lipton	8 oz*	225	1½ veg	40
Beef Vegetable Noodle	Lipton	8 oz*	225	1 veg, ½ bread	60
Beefy Onion	Lipton	8 oz*	225	1 veg	30
Chicken Noodle	Lipton	8 oz*	225	½ veg, ½ bread, ½ fat	70
Country Vegetable	Lipton	8 oz*	225	1 veg, ½ fruit, ½ bread	80
Giggle Noodle	Lipton	8 oz*	225	1 veg, ½ fruit, ½ bread	80
Golden Mushroom, Chicken Broth	Lipton	8 oz*	225	½ veg, ½ bread, ½ fat	70
Golden Onion, Chicken Broth	Lipton	8 oz*	225	½ veg, 1 fruit	50
Noodle with Chicken Broth	Lipton	8 oz*	225	½ veg, ½ bread, ½ fat	70
Noodle with Vegetables, Chicken Broth	Lipton	8 oz*	225	1 veg, ½ bread, ½ fat	80
Onion	Lipton	8 oz*	225	½ bread	35
Onion Mushroom	Lipton	8 oz*	225	½ bread	35
Ring-O-Noodle	Lipton	8 oz*	225	1 veg, ½ bread	60
Tomato Onion	Lipton	8 oz*	225	½ veg, 1½ fruit	70
Tomato Vegetable Noodle	Lipton	8 oz*	225	1 veg, ½ fruit, ½ bread	80
Vegetable Soup for Dip	Lipton	8 oz*	225	1 veg, ½ fruit	45
Vegetable Beef Stock	Lipton	8 oz*	225	½ veg, ½ bread	45

*Make according to package directions.

ITEM	TYPE OR BRAND	MEASURE	WT. (g)	EXCHANGES	CALORIES
LIPTON CUP-A-BROTH					
Chicken	Lipton	6 oz*	170	½ veg	10
LIPTON CUP-A-SOUP					
Beef Flavor Noodle	Lipton	6 oz*	170	½ veg, ½ bread	45
Chicken Noodle with Meat	Lipton	6 oz*	170	½ bread	35
Chicken Rice	Lipton	6 oz*	170	½ bread	35
Chicken Vegetable	Lipton	6 oz*	170	1½ veg	40
Cream of Chicken or Mushroom	Lipton	6 oz*	170	½ bread, 1 fat	80
Green Pea	Lipton	6 oz*	170	1½ veg, ½ bread, 1 fat	115
Onion	Lipton	6 oz*	170	½ veg, ½ fruit	30
Ring Noodle	Lipton	6 oz*	170	½ veg, ½ bread	45
Spring Vegetable	Lipton	6 oz*	170	1 veg	25
Tomato	Lipton	6 oz*	170	1 fruit, ½ bread	75
Vegetable Beef	Lipton	6 oz*	170	½ veg, ½ bread	45
LIPTON CUP-A-SOUP (Country Style)					
Chicken Supreme	Lipton	6 oz*	170	1 fruit, ½ med-fat meat, ½ fat	100
Harvest Vegetable	Lipton	6 oz*	170	½ veg, 1 fruit, ½ bread	85

*Make according to package directions.

SOUPS DRIED

ITEM	TYPE OR BRAND	MEASURE	WT. (g)	EXCHANGES	CALORIES
Hearty Chicken	Lipton	6 oz*	170	1 fruit, ½ med-fat meat	80
Virginia Pea	Lipton	6 oz*	170	1 fruit, ½ bread, ½ med-fat meat, ½ fat	135

LIPTON CUP-A-SOUP (Lots-A-Noodles)

ITEM	TYPE OR BRAND	MEASURE	WT. (g)	EXCHANGES	CALORIES
Beef Flavor	Lipton	7 oz*	200	1½ veg, 1 bread, ½ fat	130
Chicken Flavor	Lipton	7 oz*	200	1½ veg, 1 bread	105
Cream of Chicken	Lipton	7 oz*	200	1½ veg, 1 bread, 1 fat	150
Garden Vegetable	Lipton	7 oz*	200	1½ veg, 1 bread, ½ fat	130
Oriental Style	Lipton	7 oz*	200	1½ veg, 1 bread, ½ fat	130
Tomato Vegetable	Lipton	7 oz*	200	1½ veg, 1 fruit, ½ bread	110

*Make according to package directions

ITEM	TYPE OR BRAND	MEASURE	WT. (g)	EXCHANGES	CALORIES
ARMOUR DINNER CLASSICS					
Beef Burgundy	Armour	1 pkg (10½ oz)	300	½ milk, 2 veg, ½ bread, 2½ med-fat meat	325
Beef Stroganoff	Armour	1 pkg (11¼ oz)	320	½ milk, 3½ veg, 3 med-fat meat	365
Boneless Beef Ribs	Armour	1 pkg (10½ oz)	300	1½ veg, 1 fruit, 1 bread, 3 med-fat meat, 1½ fat	450
Chicken Fricassee	Armour	1 pkg (11¾ oz)	335	4 veg, ½ fruit, ½ bread, 2 med-fat meat	315
Chicken Hawaiian	Armour	1 pkg (11½ oz)	325	2 veg, 4½ fruit, 2 bread, 3 low-fat meat	535
Chicken Milan	Armour	1 pkg (11½ oz)	325	1½ veg, 2 bread, 3 low-fat meat, ½ fat	365
Cod Almondine	Armour	1 pkg (12 oz)	340	½ milk, 2½ veg, 1½ fruit, 2 med-fat meat, 1 fat	360
Lasagne	Armour	1 pkg (10 oz)	285	½ milk, 1 fruit, 1½ bread, 1½ med-fat meat, 1½ fat	370
Salisbury Steak	Armour	1 pkg (11 oz)	310	2 veg, 1½ fruit, 1 bread, 2 med-fat meat, 3 fat	475
Seafood Newburg	Armour	1 pkg (10½ oz)	300	2 veg, 1½ fruit, ½ bread, 1 med-fat meat, 1 fat	270
Sirloin Tips	Armour	1 pkg (11 oz)	310	1 veg, 1½ bread, 3 med-fat meat	260
Spaghetti with Meatballs	Armour	1 pkg (11 oz)	310	½ fruit, 1½ bread, 2½ med-fat meat, 1 fat	370

ITEM	TYPE OR BRAND	MEASURE	WT. (g)	EXCHANGES	CALORIES
Stuffed Green Peppers	Armour	1 pkg (12 oz)	340	3 veg, 1½ bread, 1 med-fat meat, 2 fat	350
Swedish Meatballs	Armour	1 pkg (11½ oz)	325	1 milk, 1 veg, 1 bread, 1½ med-fat meat, 4 fat	475
◆ Sweet & Sour Chicken	Armour	1 pkg (11 oz)	310	2 veg, 4 fruit, 1½ med-fat meat, 1½ fat	400
◆ Sweet & Sour Pork	Armour	1 pkg (12 oz)	340	½ milk, 5 ½ veg, 1½ fruit, 3 med-fat meat, ½ fat	490
Teriyaki Chicken	Armour	1 pkg (10½ oz)	300	1½ veg, 2 ½ fruit, 3 med-fat meat	370
Veal Parmigiana	Armour	1 pkg (10¾ oz)	305	1½ veg, 3 fruit, 2 med-fat meat, 1½ fat	380
Yankee Pot Roast	Armour	1 pkg (11 oz)	310	2 veg, ½ fruit, ½ bread, 3½ med-fat meat	385

BANQUET AMERICAN FAVORITES DINNERS

ITEM	TYPE OR BRAND	MEASURE	WT. (g)	EXCHANGES	CALORIES
Beans & Franks	Banquet	1 pkg (10¼ oz)	290	2½ fruit, 2 ½ bread, 2 med-fat meat, 1½ fat	500
Beef with Gravy	Banquet	1 pkg (10 oz)	285	½ veg, 1 bread, 3 med-fat meat, ½ fat	345
Chopped Beef	Banquet	1 pkg (11 oz)	310	1½ veg, 1 bread, 2 med-fat meat, 3½ fat	425
Fish	Banquet	1 pkg (8¾ oz)	250	½ veg, 2 fruit, 1½ bread, 2 med-fat meat, 4½ fat	560
Fried Chicken	Banquet	1 pkg (11 oz)	310	½ veg, 2 fruit, 1½ bread, 1 med-fat meat	355

ITEM	TYPE OR BRAND	MEASURE	WT. (g)	EXCHANGES	CALORIES
Ham	Banquet	1 pkg (10 oz)	285	1 veg, 2 fruit, 2½ bread, 2 med-fat meat, 2 fat	530
Meat Loaf	Banquet	1 pkg (11 oz)	310	1½ veg, 1½ bread, 2 med-fat meat, 3 fat	435
Salisbury Steak	Banquet	1 pkg (11 oz)	310	½ veg, ½ fruit, 1 bread, 2 med-fat meat, 3 fat	395
Turkey	Banquet	1 pkg (11 oz)	310	2½ veg, 2 bread, 1½ med-fat meat	320
Western	Banquet	1 pkg (11 oz)	310	2½ veg, 3 fruit, 2½ med-fat meat, 3 fat	515

BANQUET INTERNATIONAL FAVORITES DINNERS

ITEM	TYPE OR BRAND	MEASURE	WT. (g)	EXCHANGES	CALORIES
Beef Enchilada	Banquet	1 pkg (12 oz)	340	1½ veg, 2½ fruit, 2½ bread, 1½ med-fat meat, 1½ fat	490
Cheese Enchilada	Banquet	1 pkg (12 oz)	340	½ milk, 3½ fruit, 2 bread, 2 med-fat meat, 1½ fat	540
Italian Style	Banquet	1 pkg (12 oz)	340	1½ veg, 3½ fruit, 2 bread, 2 med-fat meat, 3 fat	605
Mexican Style	Banquet	1 pkg (12 oz)	340	2½ veg, ½ fruit, 3 bread, 1 med-fat meat, 2½ fat	485
Mexican Style Combination	Banquet	1 pkg (12 oz)	340	3½ veg, 1 fruit, 3 bread, 1 med-fat meat, 2½ fat	520
Veal Parmigiana	Banquet	1 pkg (11 oz)	310	½ veg, 1 fruit, 2 bread, 1½ med-fat meat, 2½ fat	415

ITEM	TYPE OR BRAND	MEASURE	WT. (g)	EXCHANGES	CALORIES
GREEN GIANT BOIL 'N BAG ENTREES					
Beef Stew	Green Giant	1 bag (9 oz)	255	1 veg, 1 bread, 2 low-fat meat (add ½ fat)*	205
Lasagna	Green Giant	1 bag (9½ oz)	270	1 milk, 1½ fruit, 1 bread, 1 med-fat meat	290
Macaroni and Cheese	Green Giant	1 bag (9 oz)	255	½ milk, 2 bread, ½ med-fat meat, 1½ fat	285
Salisbury Steak with Creole Sauce	Green Giant	1 bag (9 oz)	255	1 fruit, 4½ med-fat meat	400
GREEN GIANT FROZEN BAKED ENTREES					
Chicken Lasagna	Green Giant	1 pkg (12 oz)	340	1 milk, 1 veg, 2 bread, 3½ med-fat meat, 2½ fat	635
Lasagna with Meat Sauce	Green Giant	½ pkg (10½ oz)	300	1½ milk, 2½ veg, 1 bread, 1 med-fat meat, 2 fat	420
Lasagna with Meat Sauce	Green Giant	1 pkg (12 oz)	340	½ milk, 2½ bread, 3½ med-fat meat	495
My Classic Lasagna	Green Giant	½ pkg (10½ oz)	300	½ milk, 1 veg, 2 bread, 2½ med-fat meat, ½ fat	425
Salisbury Steak with Gravy	Green Giant	½ pkg (7 oz)	200	½ fruit, ½ bread, 2 med-fat meat, 1½ fat	280
Spinach Lasagna	Green Giant	1 pkg (12 oz)	340	½ milk, 1 veg, 2 bread, 1½ med-fat meat, 1 fat	370

*See EXPLANATORY NOTES for meaning of "low-fat meat" (add ½ fat).

ITEM	TYPE OR BRAND	MEASURE	WT. (g)	EXCHANGES	CALORIES
GREEN GIANT STIR FRY ENTREES					
Beef Teriyaki	Green Giant	1 pkg (10 oz)	285	3 veg, 2½ fruit, 2 med-fat meat	330
Cashew Chicken	Green Giant	1 pkg (10 oz)	285	3 veg, 2 fruit, 2 med-fat meat, ½ fat	335
Chicken and Garden Vegetables	Green Giant	1 pkg (10 oz)	285	4½ veg, ½ bread, 1 med-fat meat	230
Shrimp Fried Rice	Green Giant	1 pkg (10 oz)	285	1 veg, ½ fruit, 2½ bread, 1 med-fat meat	300
◆ Sweet and Sour Chicken	Green Giant	1 pkg (10 oz)	285	4 veg, 2½ fruit, 1 med-fat meat	280
Szechwan Beef	Green Giant	1 pkg (10 oz)	285	2½ veg, 1 bread, 2 med-fat meat	285
GREEN GIANT TWIN POUCH ENTREES					
Beef Burgundy with Rice and Carrots	Green Giant	1 pkg (9 oz)	255	1 veg, 2 fruit, 1 bread, 2 low-fat meat	285
Beef Chow Mein with Rice and Vegetables	Green Giant	1 pkg (10 oz)	285	2 veg, 1½ bread, 1 med-fat meat	235
Beef Stroganoff with Noodles	Green Giant	1 pkg (9 oz)	255	2 veg, 1½ bread, 2 med-fat meat, 1 fat	360
Chicken A la King with Biscuits	Green Giant	1 pkg (9 oz)	255	3 bread, 2 med-fat meat, 1 fat	375
Chicken and Broccoli with Rice in Cheese Sauce	Green Giant	1 pkg (9½ oz)	270	1 milk, 1½ veg, ½ bread, 1½ med-fat meat, 1½ fat	340
Chicken and Noodles with Vegetables	Green Giant	1 pkg (9 oz)	255	2½ veg, 1½ bread, 2 med-fat meat, 1 fat	370

"TV-TYPE" FROZEN FOODS

ITEM	TYPE OR BRAND	MEASURE	WT. (g)	EXCHANGES	CALORIES
Chicken and Pea Pods in Sauce with Rice and Vegetables	Green Giant	1 pkg (10 oz)	285	2½ veg, 1½ bread, 1 med-fat meat, 1½ fat	315
Chicken Cacciatore	Green Giant	1 pkg (9 oz)	255	1 veg, 1½ bread, 2½ med-fat meat	325
Chicken Chow Mein with Rice and Vegetables	Green Giant	1 pkg (9 oz)	255	2 veg, 1½ bread, 1½ low-fat meat	240
Chicken Provencale	Green Giant	1 pkg (10 oz)	285	3 veg, 1 bread, 3 med-fat meat	305
Salisbury Steak with Mashed Potatoes	Green Giant	1 pkg (11 oz)	310	2 veg, 1 bread, 2 med-fat meat, 3 fat	415
Shrimp Creole	Green Giant	1 pkg (9 oz)	255	1 veg, 1½ fruit, 1 bread, 1 med-fat meat	230
Shrimp in Creamy Herb Sauce with Linguine	Green Giant	1 pkg (9½ oz)	270	1 fruit, 1½ bread, 1½ med-fat meat, 1½ fat	330
Steak and Green Peppers in Sauce with Rice & Vegetables	Green Giant	1 pkg (9 oz)	255	4 veg, 1 bread, 1 med-fat meat	250
◆ Sweet and Sour Meatballs with Rice & Vegetables	Green Giant	1 pkg (9⅖ oz)	250	2 veg, 3 fruit, 1 bread, 1 med-fat meat, ½ fat	340
Turkey Breast Slices with White and Wild Rice Stuffing	Green Giant	1 pkg (9 oz)	255	½ veg, 1 fruit, 1½ bread, 2 med-fat meat, 3½ fat	475

SWANSON ENTREES AND BREAKFASTS

ITEM	TYPE OR BRAND	MEASURE	WT. (g)	EXCHANGES	CALORIES
Beef Enchilada	Swanson	1 pkg (11¼ oz)	320	3 fruit, 1 bread, 2 med-fat meat, 2½ fat	460
Chicken Nibbles	Swanson	1 pkg (5 oz)	140	1½ fruit, 1 bread, 1½ med-fat meat, 3½ fat	405

ITEM	TYPE OR BRAND	MEASURE	WT. (g)	EXCHANGES	CALORIES
Fish 'n Chips	Swanson	1 pkg (5½ oz)	155	2 bread, 1 med-fat meat, 2 fat	310
◆ French Toast with Sausages	Swanson	1 pkg (6½ oz)	185	1½ fruit, 1½ bread, 2 med-fat meat, 3 fat	460
Fried Chicken	Swanson	1 pkg (7¼ oz)*	205	2 bread, 2 med-fat meat, 2 fat	390
Gravy and Sliced Beef	Swanson	1 pkg (8 oz)	225	2 veg, ½ bread, 1½ med-fat meat	205
Meatballs with Brown Gravy	Swanson	1 pkg (8½ oz)	240	½ fruit, 1 bread, 1½ med-fat meat, 2 fat	300
Meatloaf with Tomato Sauce	Swanson	1 pkg (9 oz)	255	3 fruit, 2 med-fat meat, 1 fat	325
Omelets with Cheese Sauce and Ham	Swanson	1 pkg (7 oz)	200	1 milk, 1½ med-fat meat, 4½ fat	400
◆ Pancakes and Sausages	Swanson	1 pkg (6 oz)	170	2 fruit, 2 bread, 1½ med-fat meat, 2½ fat	450
Salisbury Steak	Swanson	1 pkg (5½ oz)	155	2 veg, 1 fruit, 2 med-fat meat, 2½ fat	360
Scrambled Eggs and Sausage with Hashed Brown Potatoes	Swanson	1 pkg (6¼ oz)	175	2 veg, ½ bread, 1 med-fat meat, 5½ fat	410
Spaghetti in Tomato Sauce with Breaded Veal	Swanson	1 pkg (8¼ oz)	235	2 bread, 1½ med-fat meat, ½ fat	280
Spanish Style Omelette	Swanson	1 pkg (8 oz)	225	1 veg, 1 fruit, 1 med-fat meat, 2½ fat	255

*Edible portion.

"TV-TYPE" FROZEN FOODS

ITEM	TYPE OR BRAND	MEASURE	WT. (g)	EXCHANGES	CALORIES
Turkey	Swanson	1 pkg (8¾ oz)	250	1 veg, 1½ bread, 1½ low-fat meat, ½ fat	235

SWANSON HUNGRY MAN DINNERS

ITEM	TYPE OR BRAND	MEASURE	WT. (g)	EXCHANGES	CALORIES
Boneless Chicken	Hungry Man Swanson	1 pkg (17½ oz)*	495	7 veg, 2 fruit, 1½ bread, 5 med-fat meat, ½ fat	780
Chicken Parmigiana	Hungry Man Swanson	1 pkg (20 oz)	565	1 veg, ½ fruit, 3 bread, 3½ med-fat meat, 6½ fat	825
Chopped Beef Steak	Hungry Man Swanson	1 pkg (17¼ oz)	490	3 veg, ½ fruit, 1½ bread, 3 med-fat meat, 4 fat	620
Fish 'n Chips	Hungry Man Swanson	1 pkg (14¾ oz)	420	2½ veg, 3½ fruit, 2 bread, 3 med-fat meat, 6 fat	800
Fried Chicken, Breast Portions	Hungry Man Swanson	1 pkg (14 oz)*	395	6 veg, 2½ fruit, 1½ bread, 3 med-fat meat, 6 fat	865
Fried Chicken, Dark Portions	Hungry Man Swanson	1 pkg (14 oz)*	395	1 veg, 4½ fruit, 2 bread, 4 med-fat meat, 5 fat	880
Lasagna with Meat	Hungry Man Swanson	1 pkg (18¾ oz)	530	4½ fruit, 3 bread, 3 med-fat meat, 1½ fat	695
Mexican	Hungry Man Swanson	1 pkg (22 oz)	625	½ milk, 6 fruit, 2½ bread, 3 med-fat meat, 5 fat	920
Salisbury Steak	Hungry Man Swanson	1 pkg (16½ oz)	470	1½ veg, 3 fruit, ½ bread, 5 med-fat meat, 2½ fat	705
Sliced Beef	Hungry Man Swanson	1 pkg (16 oz)	455	1 milk, 6 veg, ½ fruit, 1 bread, 2 med-fat meat	480
Turkey	Hungry Man Swanson	1 pkg (18½ oz)	525	1 milk, 2½ veg, 2½ fruit, 2 bread, 3 med-fat meat	620

*Edible portion.

ITEM	TYPE OR BRAND	MEASURE	WT. (g)	EXCHANGES	CALORIES
Veal Parmigiana	Hungry Man Swanson	1 pkg (20 oz)	565	2 milk, 4 fruit, 2 med-fat meat, 2½ fat	590
Western Style	Hungry Man Swanson	1 pkg (17½ oz)	495	½ milk, 3 veg, 4 fruit, 4 med-fat meat, 1½ fat	660

SWANSON HUNGRY MAN ENTREES

ITEM	TYPE OR BRAND	MEASURE	WT. (g)	EXCHANGES	CALORIES
Beef Enchilada	Hungry Man Swanson	1 pkg (16 oz)	455	2 veg, 3½ fruit, 1½ bread, 2 med-fat meat, 5 fat	675
Fried Chicken Breast Portions	Hungry Man Swanson	1 pkg (11¾ oz)*	335	3 bread, 4 med-fat meat, 3 fat	665
Fried Chicken Dark Portions	Hungry Man Swanson	1 pkg (11 oz)*	310	½ veg, ½ fruit, 2½ bread, 4 med-fat, ½ fat	540
Lasagna with Meat	Hungry Man Swanson	1 pkg (12¾ oz)	360	2½ fruit, 2½ bread, 2½ med-fat meat, ½ fat	490
Salisbury Steak	Hungry Man Swanson	1 pkg (11¾ oz)	335	2 veg, 2 fruit, 4 med-fat meat, 2½ fat	560
Sliced Beef	Hungry Man Swanson	1 pkg (12¼ oz)	350	1½ milk, 1½ veg, 1½ med-fat meat	275
Turkey	Hungry Man Swanson	1 pkg (13¼ oz)	375	2½ veg, 1 fruit, 1 bread, 3 low-fat meat, ½ fat	360

SWANSON LE MENU

ITEM	TYPE OR BRAND	MEASURE	WT. (g)	EXCHANGES	CALORIES
Beef Sirloin Tips	Le Menu/Swanson	1 pkg (11½ oz)	325	4 veg, ½ fruit, 3 med-fat meat, ½ fat	380
Breast of Chicken Parmigiana	Le Menu/Swanson	1 pkg (11½ oz)	325	½ fruit, 1½ bread, 3½ med-fat meat	405

*Edible Portion.

"TV-TYPE" FROZEN FOODS

ITEM	TYPE OR BRAND	MEASURE	WT. (g)	EXCHANGES	CALORIES
Chicken A la King	Le Menu/Swanson	1 pkg (10¼ oz)	290	1 milk, 3½ veg, 1 med-fat meat, 1½ fat	315
Chopped Sirloin Beef	Le Menu/Swanson	1 pkg (12¼ oz)	345	3 veg, 1 bread, 2½ med-fat meat, 2 fat	435
Pepper Steak	Le Menu/Swanson	1 pkg (11½ oz)	325	5½ veg, ½ bread, 2 med-fat meat, ½ fat	355
Sliced Breast of Turkey with Mushrooms	Le Menu/Swanson	1 pkg (11¼ oz)	320	1 veg, 2 bread, 3 med-fat meat, 1½ fat	470
♦ Sweet and Sour Chicken	Le Menu/Swanson	1 pkg (11½ oz)	325	2 veg, 3½ fruit, 2½ med-fat meat, 1½ fat	455
Yankee Pot Roast	Le Menu/Swanson	1 pkg (11 oz)	310	½ milk, 4½ veg, 2 med-fat meat, 1 fat	355

SWANSON MAIN COURSE ENTREES

ITEM	TYPE OR BRAND	MEASURE	WT. (g)	EXCHANGES	CALORIES
Lasagna with Meat	Swanson	1 pkg (13¼ oz)	375	½ milk, 2 fruit, 1½ bread, 2 med-fat meat, 2½ fat	490
Macaroni and Cheese	Swanson	1 pkg (12 oz)	340	2 milk, 1 fruit, ½ bread, 4½ fat	435
Salisbury Steak	Swanson	1 pkg (10 oz)	285	1 veg, 1 fruit, 3½ med-fat meat, 2 fat	435
Steak and Green Peppers	Swanson	1 pkg (8½ oz)	240	2½ veg, 1½ med-fat meat	180

SWANSON 3 COMPARTMENT DINNERS

ITEM	TYPE OR BRAND	MEASURE	WT. (g)	EXCHANGES	CALORIES
Beans and Franks	Swanson	1 pkg (12½ oz)	355	4½ veg, 3½ bread, 4 fat	535
Macaroni and Beef	Swanson	1 pkg (12 oz)	340	1 fruit, 2½ bread, 1 med-fat meat, 2 fat	380

ITEM	TYPE OR BRAND	MEASURE	WT. (g)	EXCHANGES	CALORIES
Macaroni and Cheese	Swanson	1 pkg (12¼ oz)	345	1 milk, ½ fruit, 2 bread, 3 fat	375
Noodles and Chicken	Swanson	1 pkg (10½ oz)	295	1 fruit, 2 bread, 1 med-fat meat, ½ fat	255
Spaghetti and Meatballs	Swanson	1 pkg (12½ oz)	355	½ fruit, 3½ bread, 1 med-fat meat, 1½ fat	410

SWANSON 4 COMPARTMENT DINNERS

ITEM	TYPE OR BRAND	MEASURE	WT. (g)	EXCHANGES	CALORIES
Bean and Beef Burrito	Swanson	1 pkg (15¼ oz)	430	3½ fruit, 3½ bread, 2 med-fat meat, 4 fat	720
Beef	Swanson	1 pkg (11½ oz)	325	1 milk, 3 veg, ½ bread, 1½ med-fat meat	310
Beef Enchiladas	Swanson	1 pkg (15 oz)	425	2½ fruit, 2 bread, 2 med-fat meat, 2½ fat	505
Chopped Sirloin Beef	Swanson	1 pkg (11½ oz)	325	½ veg, 2 bread, 2 med-fat meat, 1½ fat	380
Fish 'n Chips	Swanson	1 pkg (10½ oz)	295	2 veg, 2½ fruit, 1½ bread, 2 med-fat meat, 4 fat	590
◆ Fried Chicken, Barbeque Flavor	Swanson	1 pkg (9¼ oz)*	260	1½ veg, 4½ fruit, 3 med-fat meat, 1½ fat	525
Fried Chicken, Breast Portion	Swanson	1 pkg (10¾ oz)*	305	2½ veg, 5 fruit, 3 med-fat meat, 2½ fat	655
Fried Chicken, Dark Meat	Swanson	1 pkg (10¼ oz)*	290	2 veg, 3 bread, 2 med-fat meat, 4 fat	600

*Edible portion.

ITEM	TYPE OR BRAND	MEASURE	WT. (g)	EXCHANGES	CALORIES
Lasagna	Swanson	1 pkg (13 oz)	365	3 fruit, 1½ bread, 1 med-fat meat, 2½ fat	415
Loin of Pork	Swanson	1 pkg (11¼ oz)	320	½ milk, 2 fruit, 2½ med-fat meat	320
Meat Loaf	Swanson	1 pkg (11 oz)	310	2 fruit, 2 bread, 2 med- fat meat, 3 fat	515
Mexican Style Combination	Swanson	1 pkg (16 oz)	455	3½ fruit, 2 bread, 2 med-fat meat, 3½ fat	590
◆ Polynesian Style	Swanson	1 pkg (12 oz)	340	5 fruit, 1 bread, 2½ med-fat meat, 1 fat	515
Salisbury Steak	Swanson	1 pkg (11 oz)	310	3 bread, 2 med-fat meat, 2 fat	460
Swiss Steak	Swanson	1 pkg (10 oz)	285	1½ veg, 2 bread, 2 med-fat meat, ½ fat	360
Turkey	Swanson	1 pkg (11½ oz)	325	2½ veg, 2 fruit, ½ bread, 2 med-fat meat	330
Veal Parmigiana	Swanson	1 pkg (12¾ oz)	235	1½ veg, ½ fruit, 2 bread, 2 med-fat meat, 3 fat	485
Western Style	Swanson	1 pkg (12¼ oz)	350	3 veg, 1½ fruit, 1 bread, 2 med-fat meat, 1½ fat	425

VAN DE KAMP'S CHINESE CLASSICS

ITEM	TYPE OR BRAND	MEASURE	WT. (g)	EXCHANGES	CALORIES
Almond Chicken Cantonese with Rice	Van De Kamp's	1 pkg (11 oz)	310	2½ veg, 2½ bread, 2 med-fat meat, 1 fat	440
Beef and Chicken Szechwan with Rice	Van De Kamp's	1 pkg (11 oz)	310	1½ veg, 2 bread, 2 med-fat meat, 1 fat	375

ITEM	TYPE OR BRAND	MEASURE	WT. (g)	EXCHANGES	CALORIES
Beef Chow Mein Mandarin	Van De Kamp's	1 pkg (11 oz)	310	4½ veg, 1 fruit, ½ bread, 1½ med-fat meat	305
Chicken Chow Mein Mandarin	Van De Kamp's	1 pkg (11 oz)	310	5 veg, 1 fruit, ½ bread, 1½ med-fat meat	320
Egg Rolls Cantonese	Van De Kamp's	1 pkg (5¼ oz)	150	4 veg, 1½ bread, 1½ fat	270
◆ Sweet & Sour Pork with Rice	Van De Kamp's	1 pkg (11 oz)	310	2 fruit, 3 bread, 1 med-fat meat, 1 fat	435

VAN DE KAMP'S ITALIAN CLASSICS

ITEM	TYPE OR BRAND	MEASURE	WT. (g)	EXCHANGES	CALORIES
Beef and Mushroom Lasagna	Van De Kamp's	1 pkg (11 oz)	310	1 milk, ½ veg, 1 bread, 2 med-fat meat, 2½ fat	435
Italian Sausage Lasagna	Van De Kamp's	1 pkg (11 oz)	310	1 milk, 1½ bread, 2 med-fat meat, 2½ fat	455

VAN DE KAMP'S MEXICAN CLASSIC COMBINATIONS

ITEM	TYPE OR BRAND	MEASURE	WT. (g)	EXCHANGES	CALORIES
Beef/Cheese Enchilada with Rice & Beans	Van De Kamp's	1 pkg (14¾ oz)	420	1½ fruit, 3 bread, 3 med-fat meat, 1 fat	555
Cheese Enchilada with Rice and Beans	Van De Kamp's	1 pkg (14¾ oz)	420	1 milk, 1 fruit, 2½ bread, 1½ med-fat meat, 4½ fat	615
Chicken Suiza with Rice and Beans	Van De Kamp's	1 pkg (14¾ oz)	420	4 veg, 3 bread, 2 med-fat meat, 2 fat	555
Grande Burrito with Rice and Corn	Van De Kamp's	1 pkg (14¾ oz)	420	3 fruit, 2½ bread, 2 med-fat meat, 2 fat	535
Shredded Beef Enchilada with Rice and Corn	Van De Kamp's	1 pkg (14¾ oz)	420	4½ veg, 2½ bread, 2 med-fat meat, 1 fat	490

ITEM	TYPE OR BRAND	MEASURE	WT. (g)	EXCHANGES	CALORIES
VAN DE KAMP'S MEXICAN CLASSIC ENTREES					
Beef Tostado Supreme	Van De Kamp's	1 pkg (8½ oz)	240	3½ veg, 1½ bread, 2 med-fat meat, 4 fat	530
Cheese Enchilada Ranchero	Van De Kamp's	1 pkg (5½ oz)	155	½ milk, 1½ fruit, 1 med-fat meat, 1½ fat	245
Chicken Enchiladas Suiza	Van De Kamp's	1 pkg (5½ oz)	155	1 veg, 1 bread, 1 med-fat meat, 1 fat	220
Crispy Fried Burrito & Guacamole	Van De Kamp's	1 pkg (6 oz)	170	1 fruit, 2 bread, 1½ med-fat meat, 1½ fat	365
Shredded Beef Enchilada	Van De Kamp's	1 pkg (5½ oz)	155	½ milk, 1 fruit, 1 med-fat meat, ½ fat	180
Shredded Beef Taquitos with Guacamole	Van De Kamp's	1 pkg (8 oz)	225	1½ veg, 4 fruit, 2 med-fat meat, 3 fat	490
Sirloin Burrito Grande	Van De Kamp's	1 pkg (11 oz)	310	3 veg, 2 bread, 2 med-fat meat, 1½ fat	440
VAN DE KAMP'S MEXICAN HOLIDAY					
Beef Enchiladas	Van De Kamp's	1 pkg (7½ oz)	215	½ milk, 1 bread, 1 med-fat meat, 1½ fat	255
Beef Enchilada Dinner	Van De Kamp's	1 pkg (12 oz)	340	1 milk, 1 fruit, 1½ bread, 1 med-fat meat, 2 fat	395
2 Beef Enchiladas	Van De Kamp's	1 pkg (5½ oz)	155	1 veg, 1 bread, 1 med-fat meat, 1 fat	220
4 Beef Enchiladas	Van De Kamp's	1 pkg (8½ oz)	240	½ milk, 1 veg, 1½ bread, 1 med-fat meat, 2 fat	340
Cheese Enchiladas	Van De Kamp's	1 pkg (7½ oz)	215	1 milk, 1 veg, ½ bread, 3 fat	275

ITEM	TYPE OR BRAND	MEASURE	WT. (g)	EXCHANGES	CALORIES
Cheese Enchilada Dinner	Van De Kamp's	1 pkg (12 oz)	340	1½ milk, 2½ veg, 1 bread, 4½ fat	455
2 Cheese Enchiladas	Van De Kamp's	1 pkg (5½ oz)	155	½ milk, 1 bread, ½ med-fat meat, 2 fat	240
4 Cheese Enchiladas	Van De Kamp's	1 pkg (8½ oz)	240	1 milk, ½ veg, 1 bread, ½ med-fat meat, 3½ fat	360
Chicken Enchiladas	Van De Kamp's	1 pkg (7½ oz)	215	½ milk, ½ veg, 1 bread, 1 med-fat meat, 1 fat	245
Mexican Style Dinner	Van De Kamp's	1 pkg (11½ oz)	325	½ milk, 4½ veg, 1 bread, ½ med-fat meat, 3½ fat	420

ITEM	TYPE OR BRAND	MEASURE	WT. (g)	EXCHANGES	CALORIES
ARMOUR CLASSIC LITE					
Baby Shrimp/Sherried Cream Sauce	Armour	1 pkg (10½ oz)	300	½ milk, ½ fruit, 1½ bread, 1½ low-fat meat, ½ fat	270
Beef Pepper Steak	Armour	1 pkg (10 oz)	285	3 veg, ½ fruit, ½ bread, 2 low-fat meat, ½ fat	260
Chicken Burgundy	Armour	1 pkg (11¼ oz)	320	1 veg, 1½ fruit, ½ bread, 3 low-fat meat (add 1 fat)*	240
Chicken Oriental	Armour	1 pkg (10 oz)	285	½ veg, 1 fruit, ½ bread, 3 low-fat meat (add 1 fat)*	230
Filet of Cod Divan	Armour	1 pkg (13¾ oz)	390	½ milk, 2½ veg, ½ bread, 2½ low-fat meat	275
Medallions of Chicken Breast-Marsala	Armour	1 pkg (11 oz)	310	2 veg, ½ fruit, 1 bread, 2 low-fat meat	250
Seafood Natural Herbs	Armour	1 pkg (11½ oz)	325	½ veg, 2½ fruit, ½ bread, 1½ low-fat meat	230
Sliced Beef & Broccoli	Armour	1 pkg (10¼ oz)	290	½ milk, 3 veg, ½ bread, 2 low-fat meat	260
Steak Diane	Armour	1 pkg (10 oz)	285	3½ veg, ½ bread, 3 low-fat meat	285
◆ Sweet & Sour Chicken	Armour	1 pkg (11 oz)	310	½ milk, 3 veg, 1 bread, 2 low-fat meat (add 1 fat)*	250
Turf and Surf	Armour	1 pkg (10 oz)	285	1 milk, 1 veg, 3 low-fat meat	270

*See EXPLANATORY NOTES for meaning of "low-fat meat" (add 1 fat).

ITEM	TYPE OR BRAND	MEASURE	WT. (g)	EXCHANGES	CALORIES
Turkey Parmesan	Armour	1 pkg (11 oz)	310	1 milk, ½ veg, ½ bread, 2½ low-fat meat	265
Veal Pepper Steak	Armour	1 pkg (11 oz)	310	3½ veg, ½ bread, 2½ low-fat meat	260

BANQUET LIGHT AND ELEGANT ENTREES

ITEM	TYPE OR BRAND	MEASURE	WT. (g)	EXCHANGES	CALORIES
Beef Burgundy	Banquet/Armour	1 pkg (9 oz)	255	1 veg, 2 fruit, 3 low-fat meat (add 1 fat)*	225
Beef Julienne	Banquet/Armour	1 pkg (8 oz)	240	½ milk, 1½ bread, 2 low-fat meat	255
Beef Stroganoff	Banquet/Armour	l pkg (9 oz)	255	1 milk, 1 bread, 1 low-fat meat	260
Beef Teriyaki	Banquet/Armour	1 pkg (8 oz)	225	4½ veg, 1 bread, 1 low-fat meat	235
Chicken BBQ	Banquet/Armour	1 pkg (8 oz)	225	2½ veg, 1 fruit, ½ bread, 2 med-fat meat	295
Chicken Broccoli	Banquet/Armour	1 pkg (9½ oz)	270	2½ veg, 1 fruit, ½ bread, 2 med-fat meat	295
Chicken Parmigiana	Banquet/Armour	1 pkg (8 oz)	225	½ milk, 1 bread, 3 low-fat meat (add ½ fat)*	255
Glazed Chicken	Banquet/Armour	1 pkg (8 oz)	225	½ milk, 2½ veg, ½ bread, 2 low-fat meat (add ½ fat)*	225
Lasagna Florentine	Banquet/Armour	1 pkg (11¼ oz)	320	1 milk, 2½ veg, 1 fruit, 1½ low fat meat	265

*See EXPLANATORY NOTES for meaning of "low-fat meat" (add 1 fat.)

ITEM	TYPE OR BRAND	MEASURE	WT. (g)	EXCHANGES	CALORIES
Macaroni & Cheese	Banquet/Armour	1 pkg (9 oz)	255	1½ milk, ½ veg, 1 bread, 2 fat	290
Shrimp Creole	Banquet/Armour	1 pkg (10 oz)	285	½ milk, 2½ fruit, 1 low-fat meat	195
Sliced Turkey	Banquet/Armour	1 pkg (8 oz)	225	½ milk, 2½ veg, ½ bread, 1½ low-fat meat	220
Spaghetti & Meat Sauce	Banquet/Armour	1 pkg (10¼ oz)	290	1 veg, ½ fruit, 2 bread, 1½ med-fat meat	300

SAFEWAY'S GREAT ESCAPES LITE ENTREES

ITEM	TYPE OR BRAND	MEASURE	WT. (g)	EXCHANGES	CALORIES
Cheese Cannelloni with Tomato Sauce	Great Escapes	1 pkg (9 oz)	255	1 milk, 2 fruit, 1½ med-fat meat, ½ fat	300
Chicken Chow Mein with Rice	Great Escapes	1 pkg (11¼ oz)	320	2 veg, 2½ bread, 1 low-fat meat	280
Chicken and Vegetables with Vermicelli	Great Escapes	1 pkg (12¾ oz)	360	6 veg, 1 bread, 1 low-fat meat	275
Glazed Chicken with Vegetable Rice	Great Escapes	1 pkg (8½ oz)	240	3½ veg, ½ bread, 3 low-fat meat (add 1 fat)*	240
Oriental Beef with Vegetables and Rice	Great Escapes	1 pkg (8⅝ oz)	245	2½ veg, 1½ bread, 2 low-fat meat (add ½ fat)*	255
Spaghetti with Beef and Mushroom Sauce	Great Escapes	1 pkg (11½ oz)	325	1 milk, 2 bread, 1 low-fat meat	270
Zucchini Lasagna	Great Escapes	1 pkg (11 oz)	310	1 milk, ½ veg, 1½ bread, 1 med-fat meat	275

*See EXPLANATORY NOTES for meaning of "low-fat meat" (add 1 fat).

ITEM	TYPE OR BRAND	MEASURE	WT. (g)	EXCHANGES	CALORIES
STOUFFER'S LEAN CUISINE					
Beef & Pork Cannelloni with Mornay Sauce	Lean Cuisine	1 pkg (9⅝ oz)	275	2 veg, 1½ fruit, 2 med-fat meat	270
Cheese Cannelloni with Tomato Sauce	Lean Cuisine	1 pkg (9⅛ oz)	260	½ milk, ½ veg, 1 bread, 2 med-fat meat	285
Chicken a l'Orange with Almond Rice	Lean Cuisine	1 pkg (8 oz)	225	1 milk, 1 veg, 1 bread, 2 low-fat meat	285
Chicken and Vegetables with Vermicelli	Lean Cuisine	1 pkg (12¾ oz)	360	½ milk, 1 veg, 1 bread, 2 low-fat meat	245
Chicken Cacciatore with Vermicelli	Lean Cuisine	1 pkg (10⅞ oz)	310	2 veg, 1 bread, 2 med-fat meat	280
Chicken Chow Mein with Rice	Lean Cuisine	1 pkg (11¼ oz)	320	½ veg, 1 fruit, 1½ bread, 1½ low-fat meat	240
Filet of Fish Divan	Lean Cuisine	1 pkg (12⅜ oz)	350	½ milk, 2½ veg, 3 low-fat meat	265
Filet of Fish Florentine	Lean Cuisine	1 pkg (9 oz)	255	½ milk, 1 veg, 3 low-fat meat	230
Filet of Fish Jardiniere with Souffleed Potatoes	Lean Cuisine	1 pkg (11¼ oz)	320	½ milk, 2½ veg, 3 low-fat meat	265
Glazed Chicken with Vegetable Rice	Lean Cuisine	1 pkg (8½ oz)	240	3½ veg, ½ bread, 2½ low-fat meat	260
Linguini with Clam Sauce	Lean Cuisine	1 pkg (9⅝ oz)	275	½ milk, 2 veg, 1 bread, 2 low-fat meat	270
Meatball Stew	Lean Cuisine	1 pkg (10 oz)	285	4 veg, 2 med-fat meat	260
Oriental Beef with Vegetables and Rice	Lean Cuisine	1 pkg (8⅝ oz)	245	3½ veg, ½ fruit, ½ bread, 1½ med-fat meat	260

ITEM	TYPE OR BRAND	MEASURE	WT. (g)	EXCHANGES	CALORIES
Oriental Scallops and Vegetables with Rice	Lean Cuisine	1 pkg (11 oz)	310	3½ veg, ½ fruit, ½ bread, 1½ med-fat meat	260
Salisbury Steak with Italian Style Sauce and Vegetables	Lean Cuisine	1 pkg (9½ oz)	270	3 veg, 2½ med-fat meat	275
Spaghetti with Beef and Mushroom Sauce	Lean Cuisine	1 pkg (11½ oz)	325	½ veg, ½ fruit, 2 bread, 1½ med-fat meat	290
Stuffed Cabbage with Meat in Tomato Sauce	Lean Cuisine	1 pkg (10¾ oz)	305	2 veg, 1 fruit, 1½ med-fat meat	210
Zucchini Lasagna	Lean Cuisine	1 pkg (11 oz)	310	½ milk, 1½ bread, 2 low-fat meat	250

WEIGHT WATCHERS DINNERS

ITEM	TYPE OR BRAND	MEASURE	WT. (g)	EXCHANGES	CALORIES
Baked Cheese Ravioli	Weight Watchers	1 pkg (8¹⁄₁₆ oz)	230	1½ fruit, 1 bread, 2 med-fat meat	290
Beef Oriental	Weight Watchers	1 pkg (10 oz)	285	1 veg, ½ fruit, 1½ bread, 2 low-fat meat	260
Beef Steak in Green Pepper and Mushroom Sauce	Weight Watchers	1 pkg (9¾ oz)	275	1½ veg, ½ bread, 2½ med-fat meat, 1½ fat	340
Breaded Chicken Patty Parmigiana	Weight Watchers	1 pkg (8 oz)	225	1 veg, ½ bread, 2½ med-fat meat, ½ fat	280
Cheese Pizza	Weight Watchers	1 pkg (6 oz)	170	1 veg, 2½ fruit, ½ bread, 2½ med-fat meat	360
Chicken Ala King	Weight Watchers	1 pkg (9 oz)	255	1 milk, ½ veg, 1½ med-fat meat	210
Chicken Cacciatore, with Spaghetti	Weight Watchers	1 pkg (10 oz)	285	2 bread, 3 low-fat meat	300
Deluxe Combination Pizza	Weight Watchers	1 pkg (7¼ oz)	205	1½ veg, 2 bread, 2 med-fat meat	335

ITEM	TYPE OR BRAND	MEASURE	WT. (g)	EXCHANGES	CALORIES
Filet of Fish Au Gratin	Weight Watchers	1 pkg (9¼ oz)	260	½ milk, 1½ veg, 1½ med-fat meat	195
Italian Cheese Lasagna	Weight Watchers	1 pkg (12 oz)	340	1 milk, 1½ bread, 1 med-fat meat, 2 fat	350
Italian Style Fish Filet in Tomato Sauce	Weight Watchers	1 pkg (9 oz)	255	½ milk, 2½ low-fat meat	175
Lasagna with Meat, Tomato Sauce and Cheese	Weight Watchers	1 pkg (12 oz)	340	½ milk, 2 bread, 2 med-fat meat	330
Oven Fried Fish in Seasoned Bread Crumbs	Weight Watchers	1 pkg (6¾ oz)	190	½ veg, ½ bread, 2½ med-fat meat	245
Pepperoni Pizza	Weight Watchers	1 pkg (6¼ oz)	175	1½ veg, 2 bread, 2 med-fat meat, 1 fat	380
Sirloin of Beef in Mushroom Sauce	Weight Watchers	1 pkg (13 oz)	370	3 veg, 3½ med-fat meat, 1 fat	400
Sliced Turkey with Gravy and Stuffing	Weight Watchers	1 pkg (15¼ oz)	435	2½ veg, 1½ bread, 4 low-fat meat	390
Sole in Lemon Sauce	Weight Watchers	1 pkg (9⅛ oz)	260	½ milk, 2 veg, 2 low-fat meat	205
Southern Fried Chicken Patty	Weight Watchers	1 pkg (6¾ oz)	190	½ veg, ½ bread, ½ med-fat meat, ½ fat	270
Spaghetti with Meat Sauce	Weight Watchers	1 pkg (10½ oz)	300	3 veg, 1½ bread, 1 med-fat meat, ½ fat	280
Stuffed Pepper with Veal	Weight Watchers	1 pkg (11¾ oz)	335	½ milk, 3½ veg, 2 low-fat meat	280
◆ Sweet 'N Sour Chicken	Weight Watchers	1 pkg (9 oz)	255	½ milk, 2 veg, 1 fruit, 1½ low-fat meat	220

"TV-TYPE" FOODS, LOW CALORIE

ITEM	TYPE OR BRAND	MEASURE	WT. (g)	EXCHANGES	CALORIES
Veal Patty Parmigiana	Weight Watchers	1 pkg (8⅛ oz)	230	½ milk, ½ veg, 2 med-fat meat	210
Veal Sausage Pizza	Weight Watchers	1 pkg (6¾ oz)	190	½ milk, 1½ veg, 1½ bread, 2 med-fat meat	340
Zita Macaroni with Meat	Weight Watchers	1 pkg (11¼ oz)	320	1 milk, ½ veg, 1 bread, 1½ med-fat meat	280

ITEM	TYPE OR BRAND	MEASURE	WT. (g)	EXCHANGES	CALORIES
BIRDS EYE CHEESE SAUCE COMBINATION VEGETABLES					
Baby Brussels Sprouts with Cheese Sauce	Birds Eye	½ pkg (4½ oz)	130	½ milk, ½ bread, 1 fat	120
Broccoli with Cheese Sauce	Birds Eye	½ pkg (5 oz)	140	2½ veg, 1½ fat	130
Broccoli with Creamy Italian Cheese Sauce	Birds Eye	½ pkg (4½ oz)	130	½ milk, ½ veg, 1½ fat	120
Broccoli & Cauliflower with Creamy Italian Cheese Sauce	Birds Eye	½ pkg (4½ oz)	130	½ milk, ½ veg, 1½ fat	120
Broccoli, Cauliflower and Carrots with Cheese Sauce	Birds Eye	½ pkg (5 oz)	140	2 veg, 1 fat	100
Cauliflower with Cheese Sauce	Birds Eye	½ pkg (5 oz)	140	2 veg, 1½ fat	115
Peas & Pearl Onions with Cheese Sauce	Birds Eye	½ pkg (5 oz)	140	2½ veg, ½ bread, 1 fat	140
BIRDS EYE COMBINATION VEGETABLES					
Broccoli with Almonds	Birds Eye	⅓ pkg (3⅓ oz)	95	1 veg, ½ med-fat meat	65
Broccoli and Water Chestnuts	Birds Eye	⅓ pkg (3⅓ oz)	95	1½ veg	35
Broccoli, Carrots & Pasta Twists	Birds Eye	⅓ pkg (3⅓ oz)	95	1 veg, ½ bread, ½ fat	80
Cauliflower with Almonds	Birds Eye	⅓ pkg (3⅓ oz)	95	1 veg, 1½ fat	45
Corn, Green Beans & Pasta Curls	Birds Eye	⅓ pkg (3⅓ oz)	95	1 veg, ½ bread, 1 fat	105
Creamed Spinach	Birds Eye	⅓ pkg (3 oz)	85	1 veg, 1 med-fat meat	65
French Green Beans with Toasted Almonds	Birds Eye	⅓ pkg (3 oz)	85	1½ veg, ½ fat	60
Green Peas & Pearl Onions	Birds Eye	⅓ pkg (3⅓ oz)	95	2½ veg	60

ITEM	TYPE OR BRAND	MEASURE	WT. (g)	EXCHANGES	CALORIES
Green Peas & Potatoes with Cream Sauce	Birds Eye	⅓ pkg (2⅔ oz)	75	1½ veg, ½ bread, 1½ fat	140
Green Peas with Cream Sauce	Birds Eye	⅓ pkg (2⅔ oz)	75	1½ veg, ½ bread, 1½ fat	140
Mixed Vegetables with Onion Sauce	Birds Eye	⅓ pkg (2⅔ oz)	75	1 veg, ½ fruit, 1 fat	90
Rice and Peas with Mushrooms	Birds Eye	⅓ pkg (2⅓ oz)	65	½ veg, 1½ bread	115
Small Onions with Cream Sauce	Birds Eye	⅓ pkg (3 oz)	85	1 bread, 1 fat	115
Spinach and Water Chestnuts	Birds Eye	⅓ pkg (3⅓ oz)	95	1 veg	25

BIRDS EYE FARM FRESH MIXTURES

ITEM	TYPE OR BRAND	MEASURE	WT. (g)	EXCHANGES	CALORIES
Broccoli, Baby Carrots and Water Chestnuts	Birds Eye	⅓ pkg (3⅕ oz)	90	1 veg	25
Broccoli, Cauliflower and Carrots	Birds Eye	⅓ pkg (3⅕ oz)	90	1 veg	25
Broccoli, Corn and Red Peppers	Birds Eye	⅓ pkg (3⅕ oz)	90	1 veg, ½ bread	60
Broccoli, Green Beans, Pearl Onions, and Red Peppers	Birds Eye	⅓ pkg (3⅕ oz)	90	1 veg	25
Brussels Sprouts, Cauliflower and Carrots	Birds Eye	⅓ pkg (3⅕ oz)	90	1 veg	25
Cauliflower, Green Beans and Corn	Birds Eye	⅓ pkg (3⅕ oz)	90	½ veg, ½ bread	45
Green Beans, Corn, Carrots and Pearl Onions	Birds Eye	⅓ pkg (3⅕ oz)	90	½ veg, ½ bread	45
French Green Beans, Cauliflower and Carrots	Birds Eye	⅓ pkg (3⅕ oz)	90	½ veg, ½ fruit	30

ITEM	TYPE OR BRAND	MEASURE	WT. (g)	EXCHANGES	CALORIES
BIRDS EYE INTERNATIONAL VEGETABLES					
Bavarian Style Recipe Beans and Spaetzle	Birds Eye	⅓ pkg (3⅓ oz)	95	½ veg, ½ fruit, ½ bread, 1 fat	110
Chinese Style	Birds Eye	⅓ pkg (3⅓ oz)	95	1 veg, ½ fruit, 1 fat	90
Far Eastern Style	Birds Eye	⅓ pkg (3⅓ oz)	95	1 veg, ½ fruit, 1 fat	90
Italian Style	Birds Eye	⅓ pkg (3⅓ oz)	95	1 veg, ½ fruit, 1½ fat	110
Japanese Style	Birds Eye	⅓ pkg (3⅓ oz)	95	1 veg, ½ fruit, 1½ fat	90
Mexicana Style	Birds Eye	⅓ pkg (3⅓ oz)	95	1½ veg, 1 fruit, 1 fat	120
New England Style	Birds Eye	⅓ pkg (3⅓ oz)	95	1½ veg, ½ fruit, 1½ fat	125
San Francisco Style	Birds Eye	⅓ pkg (3⅓ oz)	95	1 veg, ½ fruit, 1 fat	90
BIRDS EYE STIR-FRY VEGETABLES					
Chinese Style	Birds Eye	⅓ pkg (3⅓ oz)	95	½ veg, ½ fruit	30
Japanese Style	Birds Eye	⅓ pkg (3⅓ oz)	95	½ veg, ½ fruit	30
GREEN GIANT BUTTER SAUCE VEGETABLES					
Baby Lima Beans in Butter Sauce	Green Giant	½ cup	95	2½ veg, ½ bread, ½ fat	120
Broccoli, Cauliflower, Carrots in Butter Sauce	Green Giant	½ cup	95	1 veg	30
Broccoli Spears in Butter Sauce	Green Giant	½ cup	95	1 veg, ½ fat	45
Brussels Sprouts in Butter Sauce	Green Giant	½ cup	95	1 veg, ½ bread	60
Cauliflower in Butter Sauce	Green Giant	½ cup	95	1 veg	30

ITEM	TYPE OR BRAND	MEASURE	WT. (g)	EXCHANGES	CALORIES
Cut Green Beans in Butter Sauce	Green Giant	½ cup	95	1 veg	30
Cut Leaf Spinach in Butter Sauce	Green Giant	½ cup	95	1½ veg, ½ fat	60
French Style Green Beans in Butter Sauce	Green Giant	½ cup	95	1 veg	30
LeSueur Baby Early and Sweet Peas in Butter Sauce	Green Giant	½ cup	95	1½ veg, ½ bread	70
LeSueur Mini Peas, Pea Pods & Water Chestnuts	Green Giant	½ cup	95	2 veg, ½ fat	70
Niblets Corn in Butter Sauce	Green Giant	½ cup	95	½ veg, 1 bread, ½ fat	105
Mixed Vegetables in Butter Sauce	Green Giant	½ cup	95	1 veg, ½ bread, ½ fat	80
White Shoepeg Corn in Butter Sauce	Green Giant	½ cup	95	½ veg, 1 bread, ½ fat	105

GREEN GIANT CREAM AND CHEESE SAUCE VEGETABLES

ITEM	TYPE OR BRAND	MEASURE	WT. (g)	EXCHANGES	CALORIES
Baby Brussels Sprouts in Cheese Flavored Sauce	Green Giant	½ cup	95	1 veg, ½ bread, ½ fat	80
Broccoli, Cauliflower, Carrots in Cheese Flavored Sauce	Green Giant	½ cup	95	1½ veg, ½ fat	60
Broccoli in Cheese Flavored Sauce	Green Giant	½ cup	95	1½ veg, ½ fat	60
Broccoli in White Cheddar Cheese Flavored Sauce	Green Giant	½ cup	95	1½ veg, ½ fat	60
Cauliflower in Cheese Flavored Sauce	Green Giant	½ cup	95	½ veg, ½ bread, ½ fat	70
Cauliflower in White Cheddar Cheese Flavored Sauce	Green Giant	½ cup	95	1½ veg, ½ fat	60

ITEM	TYPE OR BRAND	MEASURE	WT. (g)	EXCHANGES	CALORIES
Creamed Spinach	Green Giant	½ cup	95	1 veg, ½ bread, ½ fat	80
Cream Style Corn	Green Giant	½ cup	95	1½ bread	105
Peas in Cream Sauce	Green Giant	½ cup	95	1 veg, ½ bread, 1 fat	105

GREEN GIANT HARVEST GET TOGETHERS

Broccoli, Cauliflower Medley	Green Giant	½ cup	95	½ veg, ½ bread	45
Broccoli Fanfare	Green Giant	½ cup	95	1 veg, ½ bread	60
Cauliflower, Carrot Bonanza	Green Giant	½ cup	95	1 veg, ½ fat	45

ITEM	TYPE OR BRAND	MEASURE	WT. (g)	EXCHANGES	CALORIES
MORNINGSTAR FARMS					
Breakfast Links (frozen)	Morningstar Farms	2 links	45	1 veg, 1½ med-fat meat, 1 fat	190
Breakfast Patties (frozen)	Morningstar Farms	1 patty	40	½ veg, 1 med-fat meat, ½ fat	115
Breakfast Strips (frozen)	Morningstar Farms	3 strips	25	1½ veg, 1 fat	80
Grillers (frozen)	Morningstar Farms	1 patty	65	1 veg, 1½ med-fat meat, 1 fat	190
Scramblers (frozen)	Morningstar Farms	¼ cup	55	1 low-fat meat	55
WORTHINGTON FOODS					
Beef-Style (frozen)	Worthington Foods	½ cup	55	1 veg, 1 med-fat meat, ½ fat	125
Bolono (frozen)	Worthington Foods	2 slices	45	1 low-fat meat	55
Chic-ketts (frozen)	Worthington Foods	1 oz	30	1 low-fat meat	55
Chicken-Style (frozen)	Worthington Foods	½ cup	55	1 veg, 1 med-fat meat, 1 fat	135
Chik Stiks (frozen)	Worthington Foods	1 pc	45	½ veg, 1 med-fat meat, ½ fat	115
Chili (canned)	Worthington Foods	½ cup	140	1 veg, 1 bread, 1 med-fat meat, ½ fat	195
Choplets (canned)	Worthington Foods	2 pcs	90	1 veg, 2 low-fat meat (add 1 fat)*	95
Corned Beef Style (frozen)	Worthington Foods	3 slices	40	½ veg, 1 med-fat meat, ½ fat	115

*See EXPLANATORY NOTES for meaning of "low-fat meat" (add 1 fat).

ITEM	TYPE OR BRAND	MEASURE	WT. (g)	EXCHANGES	CALORIES
Cutlets (canned)	Worthington Foods	1½ slices	90	1 veg, 2 low-fat meat (add 1 fat)*	95
Dinner Roast (frozen)	Worthington Foods	2 oz	55	½ fruit, 1 med-fat meat, 1 fat	145
Fillets (frozen)	Worthington Foods	2 pcs	85	½ veg, ½ bread, 2 med-fat meat, ½ fat	230
Fri Chik (canned)	Worthington Foods	1 pc	45	½ veg, ½ med-fat meat, 1 fat	95
Fri Pats (frozen)	Worthington Foods	1 patty	70	½ veg, 1½ med-fat meat, 1 fat	175
Gran Burger (dry)	Worthington Foods	6 tbsp	35	1½ veg, 2 low-fat meat, (add 1 fat)*	105
Non-Meat Balls (canned)	Worthington Foods	3 balls	55	½ bread, ½ med-fat meat, 1 fat	120
Numete (canned)	Worthington Foods	½" slice	70	½ bread, 1 med-fat meat, 1 fat	160
Prime Stakes (canned)	Worthington Foods	1 pc w/gravy	90	1 veg, 1 med-fat meat, 1 fat	150
Prosage Links (frozen)	Worthington Foods	2 links	45	½ veg, 1 med-fat meat, ½ fat	115
Prosage Patties (frozen	Worthington Foods	1 patty	40	1 veg, ½ med-fat meat, 1 fat	110
Prosage Roll (frozen)	Worthington Foods	⅜" slice	35	½ veg, ½ med-fat meat, ½ fat	75
Salami, Meatless (frozen)	Worthington Foods	2 slices	45	½ veg, 1 med-fat meat	90

*See EXPLANATORY NOTES for meaning of "low-fat meat" (add 1 fat).

ITEM	TYPE OR BRAND	MEASURE	WT. (g)	EXCHANGES	CALORIES
Saucetts (canned)	Worthington Foods	2 links	65	½ veg, 1 med-fat meat, ½ fat	115
Skallops, Vegetable (canned)	Worthington Foods	½ cup	85	½ veg, 1½ low-fat meat, (add ½ fat)*	75
Smoked Beef-Style (frozen)	Worthington Foods	5 slices	35	1 veg, ½ med-fat meat, ½ fat	85
Smoked Turkey-Style (frozen)	Worthington Foods	2 slices	40	½ veg, ½ med-fat meat, 1 fat	95
Soyamel (dry)	Worthington Foods	1 oz	30	½ milk, 1 veg, 1½ fat	130
Stakelets (frozen)	Worthington Foods	1 pc	85	1½ veg, 1½ med-fat meat, ½ fat	180
Stripples (frozen)	Worthington Foods	5 slices	40	1 veg, ½ med-fat meat, 1 fat	110
Super-Links (canned)	Worthington Foods	1 link	55	1 veg, ½ med-fat meat, 1 fat	110
Tuno (frozen)	Worthington Foods	2 oz	55	½ veg, ½ med-fat meat, 1 fat	95
Vegetable Steaks (canned)	Worthington Foods	2½ pcs	90	1½ veg, 1½ low-fat meat, (add ½ fat)*	100
Vegetarian Burger (canned)	Worthington Foods	⅓ cup	95	2 veg, 1 med-fat meat	130
Veja-Bits (canned)	Worthington Foods	4⅓ oz	120	½ fruit, 1 low-fat meat	75
Veja-Links (canned)	Worthington Foods	2 links	60	½ veg, ½ med-fat meat, 1½ fat	120
Wham (frozen)	Worthington Foods	2 slices	45	½ veg, 1 med-fat meat	90

*See EXPLANATORY NOTES For meaning of "low-fat meat" (add ½ fat).

III. MISCELLANEOUS FOODS

ALCOHOLIC BEVERAGES

ITEM	TYPE OR BRAND	MEASURE	WT. (g)	EXCHANGES	CALORIES

Tips to Remember

1. Use alcohol only with your doctor's permission.
2. Use alcohol only when your diabetes is under good control.
3. Use alcohol in moderation.
4. Know which types of alcohol are permitted and which should be avoided.
5. Know how to count alcoholic beverages as part of your meal plan.
6. When drinking before meals, take precautions to avoid hypoglycemia.

Which Types of Alcoholic Beverages are Recommended?

1. Sweet wines and alcoholic liqueurs contain a lot of sugar and are to be avoided.

2. Beer and ale contain carbohydrate as well as alcohol. The carbohydrate is counted as bread exchanges, and the alcohol is counted as one or more fat exchanges (because, like fat, it has a negligible or slightly lowering effect on blood sugar, but is a rich source of calories).

3. Hard liquor such as gin, rum, whiskey, and vodka contains no carbohydrate but considerable amount of alcohol. This alcohol is counted as fat exchanges.

4. Mixed drinks contain the alcohol in the liquor and the sugar in the mixer (an artificially-sweetened mixer is preferable). The alcohol is counted as one or more fat exchanges and the artificially-sweetened mix is free.

How to Include Alcoholic Beverages in Your Meal Plan

ITEM	TYPE OR BRAND	MEASURE	WT. (g)	EXCHANGES	CALORIES
Ale, mild	Any	8 fl oz	240	½ bread, 1½ fat	100
Beer (4.5% alcohol by volume)	Any	12 fl oz	360	1 bread, 2 fat	160
Beer, low alcohol*	Any	12 fl oz	360	⅓ bread, 1 fat	70
Beer, low calorie**					
Bud Light		12 fl oz	360	½ bread, 1½ fat	100
Coors Light		12 fl oz	360	⅓ bread, 1¾ fat	100
Michelob Light		12 fl oz	360	¾ bread, 1¾ fat	130

*Contains half the alcohol of regular beer.

**Brands vary considerably; check labels.

ALCOHOLIC BEVERAGES

ITEM	TYPE OR BRAND	MEASURE	WT. (g)	EXCHANGES	CALORIES
Natural Light		12 fl oz	360	½ bread, 1¾ fat	110
Old Milwaukee Light		12 fl oz	360	½ bread, 1¼ fat	90
Rainier Light		12 fl oz	360	¼ bread, 1¾ fat	95
Schaefer Light		12 fl oz	360	½ bread, 1¾ fat	110
Stroh Light		12 fl oz	360	½ bread, 1¾ fat	110
Brandy or Cognac	Any	1 fl oz	30	1½ fat	70
Cider, fermented	Any	6 fl oz	180	1½ fat	70
◆ Cordials: Anisette, Apricot Brandy, Benedictine, Creme de Menthe, Curaçao	Any	⅔ fl oz	20	½ bread, 1 fat	80
Daiquiri	Any	3½ fl oz	105	½ bread, 2 fat	125
◆ Eggnog, Christmas type	Any	3 fl oz	90	1 bread, 4 fat	250
Liquor: gin, rum, scotch, vodka, whiskey	Any	1½ fl oz	45	3 fat	135
Manhattan	Any	3½ fl oz	100	½ bread, 3 fat	170
Martini	Any	3½ fl oz	100	3 fat	135
Old Fashioned	Any	4 fl oz	120	½ bread, 3½ fat	190
◆ Port or Muscatelle	Any	3½ fl oz	100	1 bread, 2 fat	160
Tom Collins					

*Contains half the alcohol of regular beer.

**Brands vary considerably; check labels.

ITEM	TYPE OR BRAND	MEASURE	WT. (g)	EXCHANGES	CALORIES
◆ Regular Mixer	Any	10 fl oz	300	½ bread, 3½ fat	190
Artificially-sweetened mixer	Any	10 fl oz	300	3½ fat	160
Sherry, dry	Any	3 fl oz	90	½ bread, 2 fat	125
Wine, dry table, 12% alcohol	e.g., Champagne, Sauterne, Claret, Chablis, etc.	3 fl oz	100	1½ fat	70

ITEM	TYPE OR BRAND	MEASURE	WT. (g)	EXCHANGES	CALORIES
Anchovy Fillets	Canned	5	20	½ med-fat meat	40
Artichoke Hearts	Cooked	½ cup	85	1 veg	30
Bamboo Shoots	Any	⅔ cup	9	1 veg	30
Bean Sprouts					
Mungbean	Cooked	1 cup	100	1 veg	30
Soybean	Cooked	½ cup	100	1 veg	30
Chocolate, bitter, baking	Any	1″ square	30	½ bread, 3 fat	170
Catsup	Any	1½ tbsp	20	½ fruit (1 tbsp free)	20
Chow Mein Noodles	Any	½ cup	30	1 bread, 1 fat	115
Chicken Spread	Swanson	2 tbsp	30	½ low-fat meat, 1 fat	75
Chickpeas or Garbanzo Beans, cooked	Any	¼ cup	40	1 bread	70
♦ Chocolate chips, semisweet	Any	⅙ cup	30	1 bread, 1½ fat	140
Cocoa, dry	Any	¼ cup	20	1 fruit, 1 low-fat meat	95
♦ Cocoa or chocolate powder sweetened	Any	1 tbsp	10	1 bread	70
♦ Cola beverage	Any	3 fl oz	90	1 fruit	40
Cornstarch	Any	2 tbsp	15	1 bread	70
Daikon	Fresh	½ cup	75	1 veg	25
Deviled Ham	Canned	3 tbsp	40	1 med-fat meat, 2 fat	170
Egg Rolls	Frozen	3 rolls	90	1 bread, ½ med-fat meat, ½ fat	130

ITEM	TYPE OR BRAND	MEASURE	WT. (g)	EXCHANGES	CALORIES
Egg Substitutes					
Egg Beaters	Fleischmann's	½ cup	120	1½ low-fat meat (add 1 fat)*	40
Egg Beaters with Cheez	Fleischmann's	½ cup	120	½ fruit, 2 med-fat meat	130
Scramblend	Land O'Lakes	½ cup	120	½ veg, 1½ med-fat meat	130
Scramblers	Morningstar Farms	¼ cup	55	1 low-fat meat	55
♦ Gingerale	Any	4 fl oz	115	1 fruit	40
♦ Instant Breakfast**	Carnation	1 cup	275	1½ milk, 1 veg, 1½ fruit	205
♦ Jams and Jellies, regular	Any	1 tbsp	20	1 fruit	40
Lentils, cooked	Any	½ cup	75	3 veg	85
Malted Powder, plain, dry	Any	2 tbsp	20	1 bread	70
Miso (fermented rice and soybeans)	Any	1½ tbsp	15	2 veg	50
♦ Molasses	Any	1 tbsp	20	1 fruit	40
Onion Rings	Frozen	⅕ pkg (2 oz)	55	1 bread, 2 fat	160
Orange Juice, imitation	Awake, Orange Plus, Start, Tang	½ cup	120	1½ fruit	60
Oriental Rice (sticky)	Any	⅓ cup	50	1 bread	70
Postum, instant, dry	Any	1 rounded tsp	10	½ bread	35
Soybeans, cooked	Any	½ cup	100	2 veg, 1 med-fat meat	130
♦ Strawberry Powder	Nestle	1 tbsp	20	2 fruit	80

*See EXPLANATORY NOTES for meaning of "low-fat meat" (add 1 fat).

**Made with skim milk.

ITEM	TYPE OR BRAND	MEASURE	WT. (g)	EXCHANGES	CALORIES
Tofu (soybean curd)	Any	2 oz pc	60	½ med-fat meat	40
Vegetable Juice, "V-8"	Campbell	4 oz	120	1 veg	25
Wheat Germ	Plain or Toasted	¼ cup	30	½ fruit, ½ bread, 1 meat	110
Yogurt					
Plain, low fat	Any	1 cup	225	1½ milk, ½ fat	145
Fruit-flavored, low-fat	Any	1 cup	225	1 milk, 3 fruit, ½ fat	225
Fruit-flavored, custard style	Any	¾ cup	170	1 milk, 2 fruit, 1 fat	205

"HEALTH FOODS"

The health food movement is growing in leaps and bounds. Since some people with diabetes may have questions, some general comments are appropriate.

Health foods are reputed to be especially nutritious. Certain health foods have even been labelled "wonder foods," capable of curing certain ailments or giving long life. Such claims are fraudulent and dangerous. The person with diabetes must rely on a physician's judgment as the sole source of knowledge concerning diet and diabetes, not on the popular press or health food promoters.

Beans, especially soybeans, have become dietary staples among the increasing number of vegetarians. Generally legumes (mature peas, beans, or lentils) contain more iron and protein than cereal grains, and the protein is of better quality. Beans also are an excellent source of dietary fiber. Soybeans are the most nutritious of all the legumes, containing more protein than most other legumes. Soybeans are high in calcium and fat. One-half cup of dry soybeans contains almost as much calcium as a glass of milk, and twice as much fat as whole milk. Soybeans are the only bean with a high fat content. Soybeans are extremely versatile and can be used as "flour," "milk," meat substitutes, and cooked beans.

Granola is a crunchy oat cereal promoted as superior to processed ready-to-eat products. Granola and other whole grain cereals are good sources of fiber. Fiber is necessary for normal bowel action and may be lacking in refined diets. Some processed cereals are notably lacking in fiber. Read labels carefully. Search for "enriched or whole grain" on product labels. Granola is a very high calorie food and contains considerable honey or brown sugar which is not recommended for diabetics. Occasional use may be acceptable. Homemade granola is easy, fun, and less expensive, but remember to limit or omit the brown sugar or honey.

Honey is generally overpromoted and very often overpriced, especially if purchased at a health food store. Honey is not recommended for regular consumption by diabetics because the body handles honey in much the same manner as table sugar (sucrose). Honey has often been recommended as a source of some vitamins and minerals, since refined sugar (table sugar) contains only calories. However, honey is a high calorie food with only small amounts of nutrients which should be adequate in a well-balanced diabetic meal plan. Honey contributes to overweight and tooth decay as much as an excess of sugar.

Molasses is another food unsuitable for diabetics (except perhaps small amounts to flavor home-baked bread) because the body handles molasses much like sugar. A by-product of sugar refining, molasses is essentially a concentrated sugar rich in iron and calcium. Blackstrap molasses, which is the darkest in color and has the strongest flavor is more nutritious than light table varieties. Molasses is certainly not a wonder food and in the normal amounts used, probably does not make a significant nutritional contribution, although molasses flavor may be highly esteemed.

Non-fat dry milk is enjoying new-found popularity as an inexpensive, handy way to supplement diets with protein and calcium. Check the label to make certain that vitamins A and D have been added. Non-fat milk powder contains all the nutrients of whole milk except the fat, for half the calories and less cost.

Rice is one of the less nutritious grains. Brown rice is certainly more nutritious than unenriched white rice and contains more fiber and trace minerals than enriched white or converted (parboiled) rice. Many people prefer the accentuated flavor of brown rice.

Sesame, sunflower, and pumpkin seeds have become popular sources of protein, calcium, iron, and B vitamins. Nuts, especially peanuts, are also good sources of protein, calcium, iron, and B vitamins as well as more common foods such as cheese, beef, chicken, and soybeans. If you can obtain seeds or nuts inexpensively, and can afford the extra calories, seeds and nuts add variety and food value.

Sprouts made from beans and seeds, although long known in Chinese cooking, have now reached the home scene. Sprouting causes a small increase in vitamin C and some reduction in other nutrients. Sprouts are very low in calories, add protein and fiber, and make an interesting menu addition.

Wheat germ supplies high quality protein, fat, and vitamin E, nutrients that may easily be supplied by other foods. If wheat germ can be purchased inexpensively, it is a reasonable additive to breads and cereals.

Yogurt is made from low-fat milk (2%) to which a bacterial culture is added. Yogurt contains essentially the same nutrients as an equivalent amount of 2% milk, unless, of course, sugar and fruit have been added. Such flavored yogurts often have twice as many calories while the protein, calcium, and other nutrients are considerably reduced. Claims that the bacterial culture is in some way beneficial to the normal intestinal organisms is controversial. Yogurt can be expensive, so perfecting a home technique can be fun and profitable.

With the exception of some snack foods and foods high in sugar and fat, all foods are "health foods." The special foods of the health food revolution make interesting additions to our usual diets and some nutritional contributions. Perhaps the major benefit of the "revolution" is in making us all more aware of the need to choose foods wisely based on nutritive value and taste, rather than on convention and convenience.

ACKNOWLEDGEMENT

The following manufacturers deserve thanks for their cooperation in supplying a nutritional analysis of their products and/or providing nutrition labels on their products.

Armour
Banquet
Best Foods
Betty Crocker
Birds Eye
Borden
Carnation
Celeste
Chef-Boy-Ar-Dee
Con Agra
Delicaseas
Dole
Dream Whip
Fleischmanns
Fluffy Whip
Franco-American
French's
General Mills
Golden Grain
Good Seasons
Gorton's
Great Escapes
Green Giant
Heinz
Hellman's
Hershey

Hunt's
Imo
Jello
Lipton
Morningstar Farms
Nabisco
Nature Valley
Nestle
Old El Paso
Pepperidge Farm
Pillsbury
Post
Quaker
Ralston
Rich's
Safeway
Sara Lee
Schilling's
Stokely Van Camp
Stouffer's
Stove Top
Swanson
Tostitos
Van De Kamp's
Weight Watchers

BIBLIOGRAPHY

Agricultural Research Service. USDA. 1976.
Composition of Foods: Dairy and Egg Products, Raw-Processed-Prepared. Agriculture Handbook No. 8-1.

Agricultural Research Service. USDA. 1979.
Composition of Foods: Fats and Oils, Raw-Processed-Prepared. Agriculture Handbook No. 8-4.

Agricultural Research Service. USDA. 1979.
Composition of Foods: Poultry Products, Raw-Processed-Prepared. Agriculture Handbook No. 8-5.

Agricultural Research Service. USDA. 1980.
Composition of Foods: Soups, Sauces and Gravies, Raw-Processed-Prepared. Agriculture Handbook No. 8-6.

Agricultural Research Service. USDA. 1980.
Composition of Foods: Sausages and Luncheon Meats, Raw-Processed-Prepared. Agriculture Handbook No. 8-7.

Agricultural Research Service. USDA. 1982.
Composition of Foods: Breakfast Cereals, Raw-Processed-Prepared. Agriculture Handbook No. 8-8.

Agricultural Research Service. USDA. 1982.
Composition of Foods: Fruits and Fruit Juices, Raw-Processed-Prepared. Agriculture Handbook No. 8-9.

Agricultural Research Service. USDA. 1983.
Composition of Foods: Pork Products, Raw-Processed-Prepared. Agriculture Handbook No. 8-10.

Agricultural Research Service. USDA. 1984.
Composition of Foods: Vegetables and Vegetable Products, Raw-Processed-Prepared. Agriculture Handbook No. 8-11.

Agricultural Research Service. USDA. 1984.
Composition of Foods: Nuts and Seeds, Raw-Processed-Prepared. Agricultural Handbook No. 8-12.

Pennington, J. and H. Church. 1985.
Bowes and Church's Food Values of Portions Commonly Used. (14th ed.). J.B. Lippincott Co.

United States Department of Agriculture. 1986.
Nutritive Value of Foods. Home and Garden Bulletin No. 72.

NOTES